TIDES OF GRIEF, WAVES OF GRACE

A MEMOIR OF SCANDAL, SOBRIETY, HEARTBREAK, AND HEALING

ASHLEY JO

For more information, email ashleyjo@thisisashleyjo.com.

ISBN: 979-8-89694-796-7 - Ebook
ISBN: 979-8-89694-797-4 - Paperback
ISBN: 979-8-89694-798-1 - Hardcover

thisisashleyjo.com

BEFORE YOU BEGIN: THE PLAYLIST

The songs you'll see woven throughout these pages
helped me survive, grieve, grow—and sometimes just
get out of bed. I hope they'll do the same for you.

Though I couldn't include every lyric (copyright
law is tricky), I created a playlist so the spirit
of the music still comes through.

Follow along as you read, or listen whenever
you like. This playlist is my gift to you.

thisisashleyjo.com/playlist

CONTENTS

This book contains memories written as I recall them happening. My recollection of events may not be entirely accurate. The human mind possesses a remarkable capacity for retaining things that serve us well and forgetting things that don't—especially in times of crisis or trauma. For the sake of privacy, many names and locations have been changed. Certain details have been omitted and some dialogue has been recreated.

FOREWORD

Adella Marie

I'm Adella, and my mom is the author of this book. I met my mom when I was born—which might shock you a bit. This book was written to tell the amazing story of her life, and I can say firsthand that it's been a roller coaster. I promise you, this story is intriguing and will keep you on the edge of your seat. Her journey is so inspiring, and it deserves to be heard by many.

Over the years, my mom has been my rock, helping me grow as a person. Our relationship wasn't always perfect, largely because of choices she made in the past. However, over the last few years, she's become one of my best friends. I turn to her for everything, including laughter; she's absolutely hilarious, and I trust her more than anyone else. We share countless moments of laughter, anger, happiness, love, and even sadness. Although our relationship hasn't always been the strongest, we continue to grow together, nurturing that special bond.

I've watched my mom transform into the incredible person she is today. During the height of COVID, she worked for a mental health program and created podcast episodes about her own struggles, while sharing conversations with others about theirs. And she did all this while juggling her own mental health, raising three kids as a single parent, working her job, and maintaining an active social life. (I know. She's pretty badass.) She is one of the strongest, most resilient people I know. Listening to her share her story was not only inspiring, it helped so many people realize they weren't alone in their pain and even motivated some to seek help.

Seeing her overcome life's challenges has shown me I can do anything. I never truly believed my mom could overcome her challenges, but here she is. Throughout this book, you may hear my name several times and learn about the experiences that shaped who I am today. I was there for many of these moments, even if I only remember a small portion of the stories she tells.

So buckle up for the roller coaster ahead. You may feel a mix of emotions—sadness, anger, lots of laughter (yes, it's okay to laugh even when you think you shouldn't), happiness, and every other feeling imaginable.

PROLOGUE

Writing your own eulogy is an odd thing to do. It's not something most people ever consider. Yet there I was, sitting at my desk, staring out my window, trying to put words to paper. The cornfield outside my window was slowly turning from green to gold as fall set in. It was beautiful, much like a part of the life I had lived. That day, however, the beauty outside of my window was a sharp contrast to the weight I felt.

I stared at the blank page in front of me. The cursor blinked again and again. How do you even begin something like this? What words do you choose when every single one feels wrong?

I took a deep breath and started to type.

Most of you who are here today know Ashley as resilient, powerful, strong. She's the one who could overcome anything, the one who would get knocked down and stand up stronger, bigger, better than most.

I paused and felt like I couldn't breathe.

That's what people thought of me, right? It's certainly what I wanted them to think.

I took a deep breath and kept going.

Many of you admire her strength and determination—you may even wish you had her courage. Many of you may wonder where it came from, how one person who has been through so much could possibly be the overcomer of overcomers.

The words on the screen blurred as my eyes filled up with tears. My hands trembled as I tried to continue typing.

Is any of this true? Or is this just the story I want to leave behind? I questioned.

I closed my eyes and reflected on the many moments that brought me here. The moments of joy. The unexpected despair. The love. The grief. The times where I wasn't sure if I would ever find the surface again. The loss. The fight to keep going when everything inside me wanted to stop.

I forced myself to keep typing.

They say that writing about upsetting events and trauma improves both physical and mental health. So maybe this story was more for me than it is for you. Maybe putting these words on paper was the only way I could make sense of it all—the loss, the calamity, the moments and choices that changed everything.

This is not a story about a perfect life. It's not a story about someone who had all the answers. But it is a story about fighting—fighting to stay above water when the waves wouldn't stop coming. Fighting to find meaning when everything felt meaningless. Fighting to believe that even in the darkest moments, there was a reason to keep going.

I didn't know it at the time, but this wasn't the *end* of my journey. It was only the beginning. So here's my story. Unfiltered. Unapologetic. And if you find yourself in these pages—if you see even the smallest glimpse of your own pain, your own joy, your own grief, your own redemption—then it was all worth writing.

PART 1

THE BROWN-EYED BOY

2007 – 2009

CHAPTER 1

THE HAPPY BIRTH DAY

Maybe they're just Braxton Hicks?

I was in the kind of labor that makes you question reality. For hours, I'd been vacillating between being convinced it was real labor and questioning whether it was really happening—the super annoying early stages of labor.

It was February 27, 2008. I visited my OB/GYN for my thirty-seven-week appointment. It was a standard visit. Dr. Smith walked in with a cheery smile on her face, asked me a few questions, and then examined me, pressing carefully on my uterus. She checked my cervix. Pausing, she repositioned me twice, rechecked, smiled, tilted her head slightly, and announced, "You're four centimeters. I think you might have a baby tonight."

I thought she was crazy. I didn't feel any pain—how could I have a baby *tonight*? But she was pretty adamant that my body was ready and that I was having contractions, whether I could feel them or not. So, I headed back to work and started walking, hoping it might increase the intensity of the contractions and kick-start labor for my second child.

I walked all day while working my teller job at Wells Fargo bank because, dammit, once those contractions had started, I most certainly wasn't going to allow them to stop. I walked around and around a set of desks for what seemed like hours, cycling back to the window in my drive-through area when customers arrived, greeting each with a smile. My coworkers probably thought I was crazy, but you don't mess with a pregnant woman, let alone a woman in (alleged) labor. I was excited, anxious, and ready to get the tough part—labor—over with. I had butterflies in my stomach, but I knew the sooner labor started, the sooner I would hold my son—a moment I'd been dreaming about for months. Although I anxiously awaited the pain of childbirth, I smiled, repeatedly touching my belly to feel the contractions harden my stomach, willing them to continue.

When I got home from work, I kept walking in a figure eight in our house. We lived in a tiny, 108-year-old home. It was quaint and somewhat falling apart, but it was absolutely perfect for what was about to be our perfect American family. Typically, when I arrived home from work, I placed the mail on the kitchen counter and picked up the random toys laying on the floor, but my nesting instinct had already kicked in, so the house was spotless. My husband, Ryan, and I had a daughter, Adella, who was seventeen months old; our second child, a boy, was the missing piece that would fill our home and make our family complete.

Placing my hand on the outside of my belly as I walked, I could feel my stomach getting hard. Dr. Smith told me to come in when my contractions were consistently five minutes apart, but they were very inconsistent and not painful—eight minutes, four minutes, two minutes, twelve minutes. I figured it was better safe than sorry, so I called and asked my mom and my sister Dani to come over while Ryan attended an evening meeting, just in case something happened. Anxiety filled me, but I was also excited about what the future held.

Growing up, I had heard my mom tell the story of my birth what seemed like hundreds of times. According to her, I arrived so quickly the nurse barely had time to check her before I popped out after three pushes, nearly shooting across the room, showing my beautiful face to the world for the first time. Because I was her second child and this was my second, I thought maybe I'd be in the same boat—the baby would arrive quickly, maybe even more quickly than I wanted him to. I loved the idea of getting labor over with, but the thought of everything happening so fast was nerve-wracking.

I was grateful when my mom and Dani arrived. We had planned for my mom to be in the delivery room with us, and my sister was there to watch Adella while we were in the hospital—every detail was perfectly in place.

Around midnight, I finally gave in and stopped walking. I succumbed to the fact that my labor was stopping and despite what my OB/GYN had predicted, I would not have a baby today.

So, I decided to lie down on the couch, watch some TV, and hopefully fall asleep. I settled on *Teen Mom* because my exhaustion prevented me from finding anything else. I had been wired all day, but shockingly, I fell asleep in no time.

Then, at 5:30 a.m. on February 28, I woke from a dead sleep and sat up straight on the couch. It felt like my uterus was in the middle of a giant lemon press being squeezed as tightly as possible, trying to wring every drop of juice out; only instead of juice, it was my baby. I gasped for air.

Holy shit, this pain is real. How on earth did I sleep through this all night?

I figured I better trudge upstairs to get my mom and Ryan to help me through this. I staggered my way up two steps, then—*boom*—a contraction hit and had me on my hands and knees on the steps. The pain subsided a little, and I felt like I could breathe again. *Whew—come on, get upstairs.* I took two more steps and another contraction hit. I was back on my hands and knees again. Breathing was always my focal point during labor, so I closed my eyes and breathed through it. The pain subsided, and I managed to plod up two or three more stairs and—*bam*—another contraction.

This time I couldn't hold it in. I had to moan through it. Not scream, like you see in the movies—I don't know if that really ever happens—but I would sigh, moan, and groan, while swaying my hips back and forth, which helped immensely.

"Ashley?" my mom called. "Are you okay?" Suddenly, she was at the top of the stairs saying, "Oh, boy, we need to go to the hospital now." I couldn't focus on anything but breathing. My mom woke Ryan up and got both of us into the car. I remember sitting in the front seat on Ryan's lap (for some reason the back of our car was full) and saying, "Oh my gosh, hurry!" I felt like I would surely have this baby right there in the car, even though we only lived three blocks from the hospital.

We pulled into the ER parking lot. The contractions were coming *fast*. I was out of it, but my mom later told me that the guy at the registration desk put his hand over the phone and said, "Get someone from labor and delivery down here now. She is legitimately having the baby, and we do not want to deliver it in the ER."

They came down quickly to bring me to labor and delivery.

"Do you want a wheelchair?" The nurse asked.

I waved my hand and shook my head while trying to breathe through the contractions. "No. There's nothing like gravity to keep labor moving."

The walk seemed like it was miles long.

Oh my goodness, did they have to put labor and delivery this far away? How many babies have they delivered in this hallway? It has to be thousands.

We got to the elevator. An old gentleman followed us in. A contraction hit, and I started moaning again. My mom looked at the man and said, "Well, do you want to help us deliver this baby?" I'm pretty sure he backed out of the elevator before the door closed. It still makes me laugh today. Poor guy.

Finally, we arrived at labor and delivery. They put me in triage, but my doctor immediately walked in, checked me, and told us we needed to move into the delivery room to have the baby. It was happening so fast—too fast. My heart raced. I could hardly concentrate—the breathing, the contractions, the people swarming in and out of the room—it was overwhelming.

Breathe. Breathe.

While I was waiting to be moved, a nurse with red hair walked in and said, "Maybe you'll have a Leap Year baby!"

My head snapped in her direction. "It's only 5:45 a.m. I better not have a Leap Year baby! I'll never survive these contractions for eighteen more hours." I placed my hand on my stomach and hunched over, hoping to find relief from the pain. The contractions were coming faster and faster.

As I was climbing into the bed in the delivery room, Ryan said, "Oh crap, I forgot the camera in the car. I'm going to go get it."

He was still half asleep, rubbing his eyes, his hair disheveled, sticking straight up in the back. A giant yawn spread across his face as he turned towards the door. His meeting had been late the night before, and I'm sure 5:30 a.m. came much quicker than he'd wanted.

My mom, the nurses, and the doctor all turned to him simultaneously with wide-eyes. "No!" They said in unison.

"Why not?" Ryan asked, squinting his eyes and tilting his head to the side.

"Not unless you want to miss the birth of your baby," one nurse said as she stared him down.

Ah, she's feisty. I like her.

In the delivery room, the baby's heart rate went down every time I had a contraction. Had I been able to think clearly, I would have been worried. All I could think about was the pain. Each time his heart rate dipped, the nurse pushed hard on my belly with both hands in an attempt to get a better reading. After my contraction, I kindly (well, maybe not quite so much) told her, "That hurts, please do *not* do that again."

Thirty seconds later, another contraction came. Sure enough, the nurse took both hands and shoved them into the fetal monitor on my belly. It felt like she was pushing and trying to force the baby out of my body. I slapped her wrist lightly as my eyes shot toward her like daggers. Whoops. "I said do *not* do that again."

"Well, you heard her," Dr. Smith said with a smile on her face. "I think it's time we switch to the internal fetal monitor."

The nurses switched over to the internal fetal monitor. With every contraction, monitors beeped because his heart rate declined. Dr. Smith looked at me with a gentle but firm smile on her face. She put both hands on her hips and said, "Ashley, the baby is a little stressed because of how quickly everything is happening. We need to get him out now. On the next contraction, I need you to push as hard as you can."

So, I gave it everything I had. Two pushes, and he was out.

He's not crying. He's purple. He is limp. Why is he not crying?

I sat up quickly, reaching my arms towards my son. "What is wrong with my baby? What is wrong with my baby?" I cried. The world seemed to pause just then; that split second seemed to last twenty minutes.

"Everything will be okay, he just needs a little help breathing because it happened so fast." Dr. Smith said. Mentally, I was panicking, but she provided the most calming presence during an incomprehensibly stressful time. She made me feel like everything was okay. Gosh, my doctor was amazing.

Seconds stretched into what felt like lifetimes. And then he cried.

Thank you, Jesus.

The sound was heaven. His cry filled the room, and it filled me.

He was small—five pounds, two ounces. His hair, a light brown with a hint of red, was so charming I couldn't take my eyes off of him. His head was nice and round, not cone shaped like most babies, because he didn't have to spend too long in the birth canal. His nose resembled his sister, Adella's, and his fingers stretched impossibly long, as if designed to cling to life with both hands.

He was perfect, and he was mine.

Cornelius John, or Case as we called him, was born exactly seventeen months after Adella. From that point on, his life continued at that pace—fast and furious, but not in the way you might think.

CHAPTER 2

THE NOT-SO-PERFECT
AMERICAN FAMILY

Before I continue forward too much further, I need to rewind my story a bit. Because to depict that we had the perfect American family would be nothing short of a lie—even though I was still hopeful that we would, someday.

Let's go back to when I was three months pregnant with Case. I'm not even sure where to begin telling this part of the story, because it's a little messy and likely a little fuzzy.

It was August 2007, and my husband, Ryan, worked at a bar a few miles down the road. A few months prior, he had sustained a back injury which caused him to be prescribed Methadone, Percocet, and Oxycodone for pain management. This pain management regimen was the perfect recipe for disaster. Unbeknownst to me, Ryan was working his way through his pills faster than prescribed, and being prescribed more than he ever should have been, likely from doctor shopping.

Looking back, it's easy to see the signs I missed. I should have known Ryan was struggling with addiction. It was an internal battle that began in his teenage years, long before we met, and by the time we'd connected, it was like a shadow he carried with him.

Before we met, he spent fifteen months in prison on possession of a controlled substance. I dismissed all of this as part of his past and viewed it as something he had overcome. Perhaps I was blind, or perhaps I was just naïve. I convinced myself I could be the reason he stayed clean, but in reality, I didn't understand addiction at all, so how could I know how to keep an addict clean? I wanted to believe he had changed, that the version of him I knew was real, but addiction doesn't let go that easily.

When Ryan took the pills prescribed by his doctor, drowsiness and grogginess took over. The look on his face became eerie, detached, and hollow. He'd slump onto the end of our black chaise lounge covered in red and orange circles, and just stare. Not at the TV, not at the wall, not at me—just through everything. His body was present, but his mind lost.

Sweat would gather in tiny beads along his forehead and upper lip, a sure sign that the drugs had taken full effect. Hours would pass, and he wouldn't move. He just sat there, in a catatonic, trance-like state. If I tried to talk to him, his responses were slow, sluggish, and delayed, if there was a response at all. It was as if I were speaking to someone in another world. He wasn't asleep, but he also wasn't awake or present for his family.

And yet, despite knowing all of this, despite seeing it with my own eyes, I convinced myself that he was just tired, stressed, and overwhelmed. A doctor had prescribed his pills, so he couldn't be addicted. Right?

The truth was, Ryan was always living on the edge. His addiction was in his DNA. Ryan wasn't just someone with a history of drugs and alcohol. Every day, he fought a battle, an internal war that only addicts and those living in recovery can fully understand.

But when you're struggling to show everyone you have it all together, like I was, maybe you just see what you want to see. Maybe it leaves you blind, unable to see the truth right in front of your eyes.

He was a bartender at night, which was the perfect job to hide his addiction. The late-night hours, the cash tips, the easy access to alcohol—it was a lifestyle designed for alcoholics to hide. And with his evening work hours, I was always asleep by the time he arrived home. When I woke up in the morning, he was usually still in bed, sleeping. I had no idea what had happened the night before and, unbeknownst to me, most nights he didn't either. Looking back, the signs were all there— red flags waving in plain sight. I either didn't recognize them for what they were, or I simply ignored them.

I was young and naïve, untouched by the reality of addiction, and I had never experimented with drugs myself. When Ryan told me his drug use was a thing of the past, I believed him. Why wouldn't I? He seemed sincere. He looked me in the eye and promised me that part of his life was over. And I, having no frame of reference for addiction, had no reason to doubt him. My understanding of alcoholism was surface-level at best. I thought being an alcoholic simply meant you couldn't drink *too* much—that it was just a matter of willpower and moderation. The naivety was profound, but I had lived a sheltered life, and there is a vast difference between knowing something in theory and experiencing it firsthand. I was about to get all the experience with substance use disorder (SUD) that I never wanted.

When Ryan ran low on his pills, he turned to alcohol. But alcohol wasn't enough—it never was—so soon enough, he found another source. His solution came in the form of an elderly cancer patient named Barbara. To me, Barbara and her husband, George, were just the sweetest, feistiest older couple I had ever met. They were friendly, talkative, and welcoming, with an abundance of life experience. But I did not know that behind those sweet smiles and engaging stories, Barbara and George were selling Barbara's Methadone pills to Ryan. Their "friendship" was enabling an addiction I was too blind to see.

I remember sitting in their dimly lit living room that smelled old and musky, thinking how lucky Ryan and I were to have met such kind-hearted people. George served as a mentor to Ryan—something he desperately needed. George had done some time in prison, but had a successful reentry into the community and had completely turned his life around. He had done well for himself. It was something my husband strived to achieve, so I fully supported George mentoring Ryan.

I did not know that every visit wasn't just about mentorship and friendly conversation. Every visit was a drug deal. Each time we left Barbara and George's house, Ryan would pocket a bottle of pills to keep his withdrawal at bay. His intricate web of lies had me trapped before I even knew it existed.

After getting to know George and Barbara, I learned that during George's time in prison, he was one of the founding members of a well-known prison gang. Ryan assured me George had cleaned up his act, shunned the practices of the gang, and completely reformed his life. It's the only reason I was comfortable with him being around my family—especially Adella.

Ryan made friends easier than anyone I had ever met in my life, a trait I was actually quite jealous of. So, I simply thought that one day he must've run into George and Barbara and become their immediate friends. This happened often with Ryan, so it wasn't completely out of character. Ryan was a charismatic salesperson who could literally sell ice to an Eskimo. He became instant best friends with many people. Too bad George and Barbara were a real life Bonnie and Clyde.

When I found out about George's prison gang history and reformation since inception, I was so intrigued that I wrote a college paper on him. Of course, that was after the initial shock set in. A colorful past didn't scare me; hence my marriage to Ryan.

When Ryan visited George and Barbara without me, he often stayed well into the night. They stayed up later than most older people I knew.

One night in July 2007, Ryan didn't come home from work. Unfortunately, at this point in time, this wasn't a rare occurrence.

Where is he? What now?

I'm sure work is just keeping him late.

No … there's more going on, Ashley, and you know it.

Don't be stupid.

When this happened, I would anxiously wait until he called or drunkenly sauntered in, trying to be as quiet as possible so I wouldn't hear him.

When Ryan finally arrived home—late the next afternoon—and woke up from a long cranky nap, he brought me up to speed on the happenings of the previous evening. I don't remember all the details of his sob story, but it involved him running from the police on foot, our car being taken to the impound, and Ryan sleeping in George and Barbara's garage all night—likely after passing out.

Here are the facts: police pulled him over for drunk driving, caught him with a 1.75-liter bottle of McCormick's vodka in his sweatpants, he took off running, and somehow he snuck into a partially opened garage, fell asleep, and the cops couldn't find him. But they found our car, his sandals, and his bottle of vodka—evidence of his crime. And they had video footage of him running away, vodka in his pants, ditching his sandals, vodka falling out, and then suddenly, Ryan disappearing.

Because they had our vehicle, the police later charged him with driving under the influence (DUI), resisting arrest, and fleeing from an officer. Being the charming salesperson that he was, Ryan showed up in court, represented himself, and got off with no charges because of the police tampering with evidence, since they picked up his sandals and the 1.75 of vodka, moving them ever so slightly to take pictures.

No joke, the judge glanced at him, glanced at the cop, and said, "I hate to do this, but, case dismissed." Ryan was remarkably convincing.

Moments like that happened far too often, and by August 2007, I was worn thin—three months pregnant, trying to keep an eleven-month-old baby girl happy, and having to constantly worry about my husband. One day, I broke.

We had gotten into an argument. (I couldn't tell you for the life of me what we were fighting about, likely money, but it's kind of beside the point.) During this heated debate, Ryan called the police. The police came over and Ryan demanded they make me leave the house.

They asked if we had gotten into an altercation, and Ryan and I both said no. Then, they informed him that because we hadn't gotten into an altercation of any sort, they couldn't force me to leave the place where I resided. When the police left, the tension didn't.

He threw my phone against the wall, shattering it and rendering it useless, while screaming at the top of his lungs, "Get out of my fucking house!" I sobbed as snot ran down my face and I struggled to breathe. This infuriated Ryan, so he took off and left on foot.

I was so fed up with the mayhem and exhausted from the pregnancy hormones that I didn't know what to do. I bawled, frantically threw some clothes into a laundry basket, strapped Adella into her car seat, got in my car, and headed to Bowling Green, Kentucky, where my parents lived.

I had no plan; I simply knew that I couldn't stay at our house anymore.

I still remember pulling into my parents' driveway, shutting off the engine, seeing my dad in the garage, and sobbing— frozen in time, unable to get out of my car. My dad looked up, and the confused look on his face said it all. I wasn't the type of kid who showed up at home without warning unless something was wrong.

We went inside. I don't remember too much of the conversation, but at one point I remember my dad referencing the Bible and stating that divorce is okay only when your spouse has been unfaithful. He said that after watching me go through what I went through, he felt Ryan was being unfaithful to me, choosing drugs over Adella and me.

I was furious. I may have even screamed. I'm not sure if it was my pride or my ignorance, but I said, "I'm not ready to throw in the towel. I am not ready to give up on my marriage. I need to keep fighting."

And so, my dad did what dads do, he helped me fight. And boy, Ryan was stubborn, so it was one hell of a fight.

We took a night to sleep, think, and pray about it. The next day, I went home and checked on Ryan. The police had been over to do a wellness check the night before, and they said he was alive, but I wanted to see for myself. I made the one-hour trek to our home in Nashville. I still remember pulling up to the house, panicking.

What if Ryan is dead? What if he is still drunk? What if he won't let me in? What if he becomes completely enraged because I am here?

It was late when I arrived, so it was dark outside. I parked in front of our duplex, walked up the path in our front lawn, and went up the front porch steps. I paused and took a deep breath.

Music was blaring so loud I could hear it from outside. I recognized it.

He must have passed out watching The Lord of the Rings. Gosh it's loud!

The volume of the music had me afraid to enter the house. I didn't know what I'd find.

But I went in anyway. As expected, *The Lord of the Rings* DVD was on the TV with the volume turned all the way up. It was stuck on the play screen. Remember the old DVDs where the play screen included a motion graphic and music? It was deafening. To this day, I still hate *The Lord of the Rings,* likely because of that dreadful experience.

I lowered the volume. Ryan wasn't in the living room. Our duplex was small, so there weren't too many places he could be hiding. I ran upstairs to check the bedrooms. There was no sign of Ryan.

I went back downstairs through the living room, into the dining room, and I passed through the kitchen. It was a disaster. Styrofoam containers with half-eaten strawberry French toast were lying open on top of the stove. A syrup bottle next to it, tipped over with syrup dripping onto the kitchen floor.

What the heck?

I opened the door at the end of the kitchen and made my way down the narrow stairs to our unfinished basement.

If you're from the Upper South like me, you're used to nice basements that are like every other part of the home—clean and finished. Not *this* basement. Our quaint home was 108-years-old. The walls consisted of exposed stone and mortar, and one wall had heaved with several cracks in the foundation. I got to the base of the stairs and turned the corner toward our washer and dryer.

Our pipes couldn't handle all the water draining from the washing machine at one time, so we had it drain into a forty-five-gallon plastic garbage can with a tiny hole and hose at the base, so it could drain slowly, in a fashion our old pipes could handle. I looked in the can; there was vomit with remnants of strawberry French toast floating in the water.

Gross.

I turned my head toward the bed that was on the floor. With our house being so old, and our bedroom being upstairs, it frequently got too warm to sleep upstairs, so we had a bed downstairs where it was cooler. There was strawberry French toast vomit on the bed too.

Disgusting.

Honestly, that's about all I remember about the trip. I don't remember where I found Ryan, but I do remember he was alive and breathing. I also remember that he refused to admit he had a substance abuse problem and wouldn't go to treatment. At some point, I conceded and drove back to Kentucky.

The next day, I drove back to Nashville and tried again. This time, I brought my dad for reinforcement.

Since Ryan wasn't willing to get the help he needed, my dad and I pursued a court order. Obtaining a court order to get someone admitted into an addiction treatment center is nearly impossible—or at least that was my experience.

To obtain a court order for treatment, you must prove that the person is a danger to themselves or others. Apparently, drinking copious amounts of vodka while taking massive amounts of Methadone and narcotics isn't enough to prove someone is a danger, despite the warning label on the bottle indicating you should not drink alcohol while taking the medication. Even today, the Boxed Warning on methadone reads: "Concomitant use of opioids with benzodiazepines or other central nervous system (CNS) depressants, including alcohol, may result in profound sedation, respiratory depression, coma, and death."[1]

Even that wasn't enough, according to the attorney we hired. We had no case. There was nothing we could do.

At that point, my dad and I decided the only way to get Ryan into treatment was to make up a story believable enough to keep him somewhere safe while we worked out the details—something completely out of character for both of us. But desperate times called for desperate measures.

We showed up at the house and found Ryan sleeping in the bedroom upstairs. We woke him up to tell him we were getting a court order to send him to treatment. We offered to find a bed for him at an addiction treatment facility if he agreed to go voluntarily. The conversation included a lot of loud voices and firm vocal exchanges between Ryan and my dad.

After what felt like hours, we finally got Ryan to agree to go to treatment. The only problem was, we didn't have a bed for him. So, we packed his things and let him think he was going to treatment, but we planned to take him to the county detox facility.

My dad and I were so excited that Ryan agreed to go that we immediately began tossing clothes into a suitcase. When we were ready to go, all we needed was to get Ryan in the car. Suddenly, he was nowhere to be found. He had disappeared. Vanished.

We spent what felt like hours searching for Ryan around the neighborhood. We checked the local casino, where he occasionally went to have a drink and chat with the bartender. He didn't turn up. Then, a neighbor informed us they saw Ryan on top of our garage. Sure enough, I looked out the upstairs window and saw Ryan standing on the garage roof with his sweatpants falling down to his knees. He was a sight for sore eyes. I stared at him, both terrified and wanting to laugh hysterically at the same time.

It was a fairly flat roof, so the fact that he was standing on it wasn't the major concern. The problem was that he was ridiculously intoxicated. One side of the garage contained a ladder—clearly how Ryan had gotten up onto the roof. On the other side, Ryan, thinking the ladder was directly in front of him, was swaying from side to side, looking as though he was about to fall to the ground with his baggy sweatpants barely hanging on.

My dad calmed Ryan and got him off the roof safely. But then Ryan decided it was time for a nap, so he climbed up the stairs, lay in bed, and fell asleep. Clearly, while we were packing for him, he had been drinking and returned even more intoxicated than when we had first arrived.

My dad was firm with Ryan that he was going to treatment, but Ryan disagreed. In the end, we got him into the van by picking him up—one arm and one leg each—and carrying him down the narrow stairway of our home. At one point, I remember Ryan pressing both of his hands and feet against the wall and railing to keep us from bringing him to the van. Looking back, I can laugh at how hysterical it must have looked, but at that moment, it was beyond frustrating.

Once he was in the car, we drove Ryan to the county detox facility and checked him in. Again, we had to tell a little white lie. The detox facility would only hold Ryan if they believed we were getting a court order to send him to treatment. Even though we knew a court order wouldn't go through based on the conversations with the attorney, we told them it was pending. Because of this, they agreed to keep Ryan for up to five days.

Leaving Ryan at the detox facility was the most disgusted I've ever felt in my entire life. Ryan sat locked in a room with a bunk bed that had a mattress about three inches thick, a sink, a small window, and a toilet that had vomit spewing out of it from *every* direction. Shit was literally on the floor. It was disgusting.

His time in the county detox facility bought me five days to frantically call addiction treatment centers, hoping to find someone with an open bed willing to admit Ryan. This proved to be more difficult than I had expected because Ryan's Methadone addiction meant he was taking a drug many addiction treatment centers use to get people off of drugs— something many local facilities didn't have experience with and thus were not comfortable handling.

After several rounds of hopeless calls, I found a facility willing to take Ryan. They had one condition: they required me to have a medical doctor oversee Ryan's care while he was in treatment. The doctor needed to be available at any moment should something go wrong with Ryan's detox. Just when I thought I'd overcome the biggest obstacle, an even bigger one appeared.

I called several doctors, and no one would work with Ryan. Finally, I made one of the weirdest phone calls of my life. I called the doctor who originally prescribed Ryan the medication. I now know this doctor is simply a drug dealer in a white coat. When I reached the doctor's office, the nurse wouldn't allow me to speak to the doctor. Of course, I knew this would be the case. However, after explaining to the nurse that my husband had become addicted to the medication he prescribed, likely because of overprescription, and I would report him to the authorities if she didn't get him on the phone immediately, she promptly got the doctor. He agreed to oversee Ryan's treatment program.

After five days in the county detox facility, Ryan could think with a rational mind. He decided to "voluntarily" enter the treatment program. I use voluntarily in quotes because he was likely convinced to do so because we told him we were getting a court order—he didn't realize that was a dead end. When my dad and I picked him up from the county detox, he requested we stop at a local grocery store, so that he could get a few things for treatment. He needed a new toothbrush. Later, I found out that he stole a bottle of vodka and consumed it in the bathroom, knowing if he hadn't, he would have never followed through. The only way to show up at rehab was drunk or hungover—it's an unspoken rule.

Ryan spent thirty days in treatment. During his time in the program, the full truth about George and Barbara came out at one of our family counseling sessions.

"Ashley, I need to tell you something because part of this program of recovery is making amends," Ryan said.

I braced myself, preparing for the worst-case scenario.

"George and Barbara aren't who you think they are," he said.

I nodded, as if to get him to keep going, gesturing to him to continue telling the story.

"As you know, George was the founder of a prison gang—a pretty dangerous one at that. He's done some not-so-great things in life. But what you didn't know is that George wasn't really mentoring me, he was selling to me. George and Barbara were my drug dealers. When we visited them, I bought pills from Barbara. She hated the way they made her feel, so she sold them to me. When I ran out and she didn't have more to sell, George told me which doctor to see and what to say to get the maximum allowed prescription for Methadone."

"What?" I said in disbelief, crossing my arms before throwing my head into my hands. I glanced over at Ryan's counselor. He tried keeping a straight face.

I thought you said he had changed?! Reformed? Yet still selling drugs?

Was his reformation story simply a cover?

George babysat my daughter! He's your drug dealer? He's the reason we're here?

"You're kidding me, right?"

With the lies I had been told, I'd looked past the prison gang history. I was a sucker for a Saul to Paul transformation story. But I couldn't look past George and Barbara being his drug dealers. I made him promise he would *never* speak to them again.

Thirty days later, Ryan exited treatment sober and committed to attending twelve-step recovery meetings every single day for the next year. He attended his first post-treatment meeting less than an hour after he was home—demonstrating his commitment to Adella and me.

When Case was born, Ryan was five months sober. His sobriety constantly occupied space in my mind, and I lived every day fearing he might relapse.

All that to say, our family was anything but the perfect American family.

CHAPTER 3

THE DIAGNOSIS

Now that I've set the record straight about being the not-so-perfect American family, we can get back to the rest of the story.

Case was two months old, and I loved the baby stage, so I was soaking it all up. Ryan and I were big fans of *The Happiest Baby on the Block* by Harvey Karp, M.D. After taking a class on it, we implemented the Five S's—swaddling, side or stomach, shushing, swinging, sucking—to a T. Case wore the title "happiest baby on the block" very well.

I produced milk like a cow, so breastfeeding came easily for both of us. My freezer was full of milk, every new mother's dream. Given Ryan's past, his sobriety was nothing short of a miracle. Case was a wonderful baby, and Adella adored her new sibling (as much as a nineteen-month-old can). Things were going well.

During Case's second month, I remember changing his diaper, and when I lifted his legs up, they would just plop back down onto the changing table with a thud. I thought it was weird, but I chalked it up to him being a relaxed baby. In utero,

Adella had been a gymnast, kicking my ribcage so hard, it was likely bruised inside. Case was never like that. He would kick, but they were light, gentle kicks. From the time I felt the first kick, I knew that Case was a relaxed, laid-back baby.

During his two-month well-baby check, the pediatrician asked me if he would ever bear weight on his legs.

I think so? Wait, no. He doesn't. Ever. Gosh, that's weird. I hope that's not concerning. I hope there is nothing wrong.

(Side note: my brain frequently goes on incessant rants. I have hundreds and thousands of thoughts floating around my mind at any given time. The thoughts are louder when crisis and trauma abound.)

"Sometimes," I said, with hesitancy in my voice. "Maybe ... I don't know. Now that you say it, I'm not really sure."

Gosh, what kind of mother am I? I don't know if my child can bear weight on his legs.

He seemed like a normal baby until that moment. He just seemed relaxed.

The pediatrician, Dr. Carina Warner, said that it was probably nothing, but we'd want to get him tested for a few things—specifically hip dysplasia and muscular dystrophy.

What the heck? You think my kid might have muscular dystrophy? He will be in a wheelchair.

Case was born with a minor cleft earlobe. Until then, that was the worst thing that had happened to him. When he was first born, my mom and her friend took his newborn baby pictures. They included close-up pictures of his cleft ear. I was furious when I saw the pictures. I was worried that kids would make fun of the way my kid's ear looked, probably caring about looks a little too much. I was worried he wouldn't get a date to the prom. Had Case been a girl, it would have been so much easier to cover up with long hair.

Oh, how I regret those thoughts now; how simple a tiny ear deformity is in the grand scheme of life.

But back to the story ...

Screw the way his ear looks; now he certainly won't get a date to the prom. No girl is going to fall in love with my son if he's in a wheelchair.

Yes, my brain went on another tangent, but externally, I held it together.

They drew blood to test Case for muscular dystrophy and took some x-rays to test for hip dysplasia. The tests came back quickly. It was not muscular dystrophy. Thank God. In my mind, that was the worst-case scenario. The pediatrician put us on a waiting list to see a pediatric neurologist for the next round of tests. We scheduled an appointment for three months down the road. It seemed like a long wait, but I knew that meant this was one of the best doctors around, and my kid didn't have muscular dystrophy, so I wasn't all that concerned. I could go back to life without worrying about my child being confined to a wheelchair for eternity.

We continued on with our normal lives for the next three months. Twelve days before my twenty-third birthday, I took Case to the pediatric neurologist. Ryan was on a mission trip in Los Angeles, California with some of his sober friends, and Adella was at daycare, so it was just Case and me.

The neurologist, Dr. Betsy Blunch, a stout older woman who looked wise beyond her years, asked me a lot of standard doctor questions about Case's development. It seemed like a pretty normal appointment to me.

She took Case in her arms to examine him. She lifted him up in the air, smiled at him, and spoke to him in a cooing, friendly (baby) voice. Turning to me, she said, "Does his tongue always quiver like that?"

Does my kid's tongue quiver? What kind of question is that? I don't know. Oh my goodness, I don't know that my kid's tongue quivers nonstop. What kind of mother am I? A horrible one?

The thoughts in my mind were incessant ... they needed to stop.

"I don't know, maybe," I said, with an extreme amount of hesitancy in my voice. "Now that you say it, I actually think it does, but I've never thought about it before today."

What I actually wanted to say was, "Is that bad?" But I held it all together on the outside and continued squirming internally, second guessing every word that came out of my mouth.

I remember her laying him on the bench in the room. She played with his legs a bit, lifted his arms, and continued talking to him in a friendly, baby voice. Then, she said something I'll never forget, in the calmest, most reassuring tone: "Ashley, I am going to test Case for something today and only one thing. It's not a great disease to have, so please don't go home and research it."

Do you know me? I am the queen of research. Of course, I'm going to research it.

Instead, I gave a grim smile and said, "Okay."

"It's called spinal muscular atrophy, or SMA, and it isn't a great disease to have. There are three different types of spinal muscular atrophy. Type 1 is usually diagnosed before the child is six months old, Type 2 is most often diagnosed between six months and two years old, and Type 3 can be diagnosed into adulthood. Since Case is five months old, he is right on the cusp of possibly being Type 2, but since you've noticed symptoms for the last few months, it's more likely that he's a Type 1. If he were to have Type 1 SMA, there's only a 50 percent chance he would live to see his second birthday and a near inevitable death before reaching adulthood."

My head spun around and around. She was still talking, but I could no longer hear the words coming out of her mouth. I frantically floated in and out of a dissociated state. I could see that her lips were moving, but all I could hear was a ringing in my ears as the world around me began to spin.

"I'll step out to get the nurse. She will come in and draw some blood, and it will take two to eight weeks for us to get the results back," Dr. Betsy said.

As she stepped out of the room, I frantically typed "spinal muscular atrophy" into my phone so I wouldn't forget what it was called.

Wow, I wish I hadn't come to this appointment alone. Also, excuse me? Did you say two to eight weeks? You want me to wait two to eight weeks to find out if my child has a 50 percent chance of living to see his second birthday? What kind of cruelty is that?

The nurses came in, drew Case's blood, then the doctor came back and told me that if the results were positive for SMA, she would call me and ask me to come into the office to discuss them. If the results were not positive for SMA, her office would call me to schedule an appointment for another round of testing. It was completely and utterly overwhelming and devastating at the same time.

I remember walking out, but I'm not even sure if I stopped at the front desk. I was numb.

I got to my car on the fifth floor of the parking garage of the Centennial Children's Hospital. My car was facing east on the very edge of the garage. It was dark and gloomy. It felt like a scene from a movie where something bad is definitely about to happen. I sat in my car for what felt like hours, paralyzed, unsure of what to do next.

Breathe, Ashley. Breathe.

Finally, I picked up the phone and called my mom. My mom and I had a unique relationship, so I didn't call her too often, but she was always there for me whenever I needed her, and this definitely was a moment for a phone call to my mom.

She answered, "Hi Ashley," with her typical cheery, friendly voice.

I stared blankly at the cement wall in front of me. I was numb. I didn't say anything.

"Ashley?"

I opened my mouth and tried to talk, but words wouldn't come out. Then suddenly I erupted into tears and shared all the details of the appointment that I could remember.

"What's the disease called?" She asked.

"I don't even remember. I need to look at my phone," I said. "All I know is that they are going to call me on my birthday and tell me my baby is going to die."

"Ashley, your birthday is in twelve days. They said the test would take two to eight weeks. They aren't going to call you on your birthday."

But I was certain they would. I'd never been more certain of anything in my life. I can't explain it. Some call it intuition. Some call it a gut feeling. I call it *God*.

Eventually, I hung up and looked at the note I had typed on my phone.

Spinal muscular atrophy.

I read it over and over again. Eventually, I started the car and drove home.

Ryan is only ten months sober. How is he going to handle this news? My life is going to fall apart. What are we going to do? I am not ready for this.

When I got home, I went downstairs, sat at my computer desk in the basement, and typed "spinal muscular atrophy" into the Google search engine. I sat for hours and read page after page about SMA. A few phrases kept sticking out to me.

For Type 1 SMA, the most severe form, "Symptoms begin at birth or within the first six months of life."[2]

Crap, we noticed Case's symptoms when he was two months old.

The next series of words that hit me like a freight train were, "Frog-like posture" and "bell-shaped chest."[3]

Now that I read that, Case does have frog-like legs and a bell-shaped chest.

And then, the kicker: "Without breathing support, children with type 1 SMA die before their second birthday."[4]

What happened to 50 percent?

I tried not to panic, but it was semi-inevitable. How do you not panic when you've been told your son may die?

My next thought immediately went to Ryan and his early sobriety. There was no way he would be able to handle news like this. I didn't know what to do, so I reached out to his friend, Scott, from the program for guidance and direction. We spoke to Ryan together when he was home from the mission trip.

Ryan took it much better than I thought he would. He maintained a positive attitude. Once we were both fully informed, the treacherous wait began. We had to continue on with life until the phone rang, telling us what to do next. The wait was miserable.

Even in the midst of such agony, there were countless moments of joy—tiny moments that I clung to like lifelines. Believing you're about to receive an impending death sentence for your child has this funny way of putting everything into perspective. The insignificant moments of daily life faded into the background, and I found myself cherishing things I had once taken for granted. Every single diaper change became a gift. The warmth of his body snuggled against mine, the way his tiny fingers curled around mine—it all felt fleeting, too precious to take for granted.

Every evening, after Adella went to sleep, I'd settle into the black La-Z-Boy rocking chair in Case's nursery. In the glow of the nightlight, I'd hold him close, listen to him breathe, and watch the slow rise and fall of his chest as I sang him to sleep. It became our routine—those twenty to thirty minutes when the world around us disappeared. It was just the two of us wrapped in music.

"You Are My Sunshine" was always first, followed by "The B-I-B-L-E" and "Deep and Wide"—songs from my childhood that carried the comfort of familiarity. Then there was "Lullabye" by Billy Joel, a song I had always loved, yet never fully realized the weight of until much later. The lyrics talk about how temporary life is and how eventually we'll all be gone, but lullabies continue forever.

It wasn't until later that I recognized the irony, singing about Case's future. It was a lullaby that was preparing us both for an inevitable goodbye.

Then, there were the songs that belonged only to us—the ones I made up just for my kids. They were simple; they were sweet, and they were my favorite.

I love you, Cornelius, you're my favorite friend

I love you from beginning to end

I love you, Cornelius, you're my favorite friend

I love you.

I love you, I love you, I love you, I love you

I love you, Cornelius, you're my favorite friend

I love you.

I sang the song over and over, hoping the words and Case could stay with us forever. I never wanted to forget the moment. Every evening in that nursery, my world stopped spinning just for a moment.

Then, before I placed him gently in his crib, I'd lean down and kiss his forehead. I would inhale deeply—taking in his perfect baby scent, knowing that one day, it would be nothing more than a memory. I wanted to smell his scent forever. I never wanted to forget.

The routine became my anchor, more for me than for Case. Singing was my safe place, my way of holding onto something when everything else felt like it was slipping away. As a child, my parents had taught me the power of music from the very beginning—to inspire, to heal, to comfort you when the world around you was falling apart. And in those quiet, dark moments, singing to my son was the only way I knew how to keep myself—*our family*—from breaking.

CHAPTER 4

THE PHONE CALL

Despite it being my twenty-third birthday, July 28, 2008, was a normal day at work. I sat chatting with my co-workers Jen, Tim, and Susie as I normally would throughout the day. I helped customers with a friendly voice and a smile on my face. But in the back of my mind, I was anxiously waiting for the phone to ring.

I received constant reassurance from my family and friends that my gut instinct was not correct. They told me there was no way the doctor would call with Case's SMA test results on my birthday—especially since they said the test would take two to eight weeks.

Since it was 4:25 p.m., I prepared to leave for the day. Everyone was probably right. I finally felt like I could breathe a sigh of relief. I had to count and audit my till before I could leave, a task I completed daily.

At 4:30 p.m. on the dot, I heard the phone ring. My mind instantly went on high alert. Tim picked it up. He was the nicest gentleman you could ever meet, with a heart of gold. The entire team at the bank knew I had been waiting all day for the dreaded phone call. They had also assured me I would not receive a call, and if I did, it would be good news. There were positive vibes all around—positive vibes from everyone, except me. I remained convinced the doctor would call today and give me a death sentence for my son. Definitely not positive news.

Then I heard Tim say, "Ashley, the phone is for you."

My heart sank to my feet. Below my feet, actually. I'm pretty sure my heart was in the ground beneath me, that it had stopped completely, and I was no longer alive. Time stopped.

I snapped back into reality, realizing I had left my cash drawer open with all the money exposed—a huge no-no at the bank. Quickly, I turned toward the phone facing the bank lobby, nearly lunging for it.

"Hello, this is Ashley," I said semi out of breath.

"Hello Ashley, this is Dr. Betsy Blunch from Centennial Children's Hospital. We received Cornelius' test results, and I'd like to meet with you and your husband. How soon can you be here?"

Meet with me and my husband? Oh shit, she told me that if the results were positive, she would call me and ask me to come into the office to discuss the results. How soon can I be there? You want to meet today? Oh my goodness. I'm freaking out.

"How soon can we be there today?" There was hesitation in my voice.

Am I hearing her right?

"Yes, today. I just wrapped up seeing patients and I'll be doing paperwork into the early evening. Are you able to make it in tonight?" Dr. Betsy said.

"Yes, let me get a hold of my husband and we'll be right in. We'll do the best we can to be there by 5:00."

"Ok. When you get here, just tell them you are here to meet with Dr. Betsy. We'll see you soon."

I hung up the phone. My world started spinning.

"I've gotta go," I said to Tim, Jen, and Susie.

"Go! Go!" Susie said as she waved her hand quickly towards the door. She was an amazing manager. The entire team at the bank was rooting for me and my family.

I sprinted out of the bank with my till still open. Something I probably could have gotten in trouble for in the long run, but again, Susie was the best.

I jumped into my car, grabbed my cell phone, and called Ryan.

No answer.

Of all the days, Ryan. Pick up your phone. This is important, and you knew this call could be coming.

I called again, and again, and again as I drove home. No answer. I tried his office line. Same result.

Oh my gosh, you're killing me. Please answer your phone. I guess I'll be going by myself ... again.

Eventually, I found the phone number of one of Ryan's colleagues and old roommates. I knew they worked at the same company, but they weren't in the same division. Regardless, he got a hold of Ryan and let him know he needed to meet me at home as soon as possible.

I made it home before him and realized I didn't know if we were supposed to bring Case to the appointment. Feeling a bit lost and ashamed for not asking, I called Centennial Children's. The receptionist put me on a brief hold, came back, and said, "I spoke with Dr. Betsy, and she said there's no need to bring Cornelius to the appointment."

What? Why not? Are you telling me you cannot do anything for him? Isn't there medication, therapy, or treatment? Surely there must be something you can do.

"Ok," I said. "Thank you."

I didn't know what to do, so I changed my clothes. When I'm in moments of chaos and panic, I look for anything I can control to feel safe. At that moment, the only thing I could control was how I looked. I'd never felt so utterly helpless in my life.

I put on three different outfits, hating each one more than the last. I landed on a black frilly mini-skirt and a white burnout t-shirt with two fire-breathing dragons on it. To this day, I will never forget the outfit I wore. It may seem insignificant, but the sight of myself in the mirror is something I will never forget. I see into the darkness of my eyes—the fear, the worry, the sheer terror. Headed to receive a death sentence for my son, all that I could think about was, *is this what you want to be wearing when they tell you your kid is going to die?* It was likely a way to escape the mental agony I was facing.

We were supposed to go to Bowling Green that night for a birthday party for my grandpa Grant and me. I texted my family to tell them we would probably be late, and why.

Ryan finally came home. It was the longest thirty-minute wait of my life. It felt like days. We got in the car, made the short drive to Centennial Children's, and walked into the clinic. They immediately took us back to Dr. Betsy's office.

Well, this must not be good. We got to bypass the waiting room. That has never happened before.

When Dr. Betsy walked into the room, she delivered the news I thought she would deliver. Case's test results came back positive for SMA.

What. The. Fuck.

Despite everything I had read online, she was actually quite positive throughout the meeting and said we wouldn't know until Case continued to progress whether he was Type 1 or Type 2. We left with three appointments with specialists—a pulmonologist, a genetic counselor, and a physical therapist—and a sleep study scheduled.

We clung to the hope that maybe, just maybe, Case had Type 2 SMA. Children with Type 2 SMA may sit up, but they can't walk. And while that significantly impacts their lives, they can live well into adulthood. This didn't seem so bad.

I left feeling a bit of hope with no action steps other than a series of doctor's appointments. It seemed this was going to be the new normal—doctors, hospitals, medical bills, big words I couldn't pronounce—a world I knew very little of but was about to get indoctrinated into.

We stopped at the daycare on the way home from the doctor's office to pick up Adella and Case, loaded up the car, and headed to my twenty-third birthday party.

Happy freaking birthday.

My family had reserved the back room at Godfather's Pizza in Bowling Green for the party. We knew we were about to rain on everyone's birthday parade by sharing the news, so we decided to wait until after we finished eating. Only, I couldn't eat. My pizza sat untouched while I held Case and stared off into the distance wondering what our life was about to become. I couldn't think clearly, let alone eat anything. I didn't want the moment to end. Moving from that moment to the next meant it was real, and I didn't want it to be real. I didn't want it to be my life. It wasn't fair. My entire family was making small talk while all I could think was: *My kid is going to die. My husband is going to relapse. How am I going to survive?*

I don't remember who shared, me, Ryan, or one of my parents. I think it may have been my dad who shared the news with our extended family. I had tears streaming down my face, and I looked over at my Grandpa Grant to see tears streaming down his face too.

I can still see the back room of Godfather's. I can still see the chair I was sitting in, still feel the warm tears streaming down my face when I didn't want to cry. I hated crying. But mostly, I can still see the tears streaming down the face of the biggest, boldest, strongest man that I knew. It was the first and only time I ever saw my Grandpa Grant cry.

My family was amazing. They prayed over all of us. I was so hot when they prayed—hives broke out all over my chest. After the prayer, I saw my Aunt Lora talk to my Uncle Dave for a moment. Then, they walked over to Ryan and me and told us they would like to purchase a professional photoshoot for our family with their family friend who was an amazing photographer. To this day, I cherish those pictures more than they may ever know.

The first hard part was over—we told the first group of people. Uttering the words, "Case has spinal muscular atrophy, and he might die," was so hard, but we survived. And, if we did it once, we could do it again.

CHAPTER 5

THE PULMONOLOGIST

The appointment with the pulmonologist was the first of three important appointments. Dr. Michael Lindwell, a top pulmonologist in the area, greeted us with a firm handshake then sat down on his black stool. He was a thin, bald, white man wearing glasses. He seemed kind, yet direct and to the point. His directness allowed us to realize this visit wouldn't be as positive as our visit with Dr. Betsy. Apparently, the neurologist left the pulmonologist to deliver the harshest news, and I say that with the utmost respect—I wouldn't want to be the bearer of devastating news either.

Dr. Michael explained many things we already knew about SMA. Doctors typically diagnose Type 1 before six months of age, Type 2 before the age of two, and Type 3 well into adulthood.

"Because you've seen symptoms in Case since he was two months old, it is likely he has Type 1 spinal muscular atrophy," he said.

Ouch. That hurt.

He explained that the muscles in the body gradually weaken and atrophy in SMA. The diaphragm, being a muscle, would eventually struggle to function. At one point, he rolled his chair back, put his hands on his knees, and paused.

He's thinking really hard about what he's about to say next.

Then he said, "This is the hardest thing I have to tell parents. Your son will almost certainly die before you. Unless there is a tragic accident or lightning strikes, there is nearly a 100 percent chance your son will die before you."

And with those words, hope slipped away. Any glimmer of hope had been a cruel illusion. I wished they had been honest from the very beginning. False hope just made things worse.

Despite the lack of comforting words, Dr. Michael's presence was reassuring. He knew what he was talking about. He had walked this road with other parents and understood the journey we were about to embark on. This brought Ryan and me a tremendous amount of relief.

He meticulously outlined signs to watch for indicating that Case was in respiratory distress or having difficulty breathing. Retracting lungs. Nose flaring. Pale, ashen skin. Fast or shallow breathing. All things that seemed terrifying, to say the least. He discussed three approaches to SMA care: invasive, noninvasive, and palliative. He also mentioned he was eager to see the results of Case's upcoming sleep study, which would show if there were periods during the night when Case stopped or had trouble breathing.

We asked about treatments or therapies, and he said, "Nothing right now. We just have to wait and see what happens."

So, we left another doctor's appointment with more answers, but even less hope. There was no form of preventative treatment, and as a mom, that's heart wrenching, frustrating, and impossible to accept. All we could do now was rely on prayer, the support of our community, and the leadership of his medical team.

Our church family was amazing. We started attending The Refuge when Case was about two months old. It was a church filled with authenticity, welcoming people with open arms. Being just a few months sober when we first started attending, Ryan felt right at home. I grew up going to church, so I was just happy we had found somewhere we could call home. Their amazing worship through music kept me going. We shared the news with our church family, prayed, and waited, trying to enjoy every moment with Case and Adella.

The night of the sleep study finally arrived, and I was eager to get it over with. Ryan stayed home with Adella while I took Case to the sleep study so I could nurse him throughout the night.

We arrived, and they connected hundreds of wires to his head and chest, put him in a crib, and told me to wait in an uncomfortable blue chair until he fell asleep. The uncomfortable blue chair was apparently my bed for the night. I was just grateful I had a place to lay my head and try to sleep.

The night was miserable. It was clear from the very first hour that Case was very uncomfortable. He kept grimacing and moaning. I thought he was uncomfortable because of all the wires. As an adult, I cannot imagine trying to sleep like that—attached to hundreds of wires.

At one point, the technician came in and told me Case's oxygen level was only eighty-eight. They asked if that was normal and what they should do.

Is that normal? I don't know. What should they do?

"I don't know," I replied.

We never received results from the sleep study because Case didn't sleep. Poor baby Case was up all night, and so was I— horrified by what I was witnessing, feeling like my world was slipping through my fingers. Exhausted and scared, I drove home and decided the best thing for both of us would be to go to bed. I thought maybe if Case was in his own bed, he could sleep.

Looking back, the mom in me knew I should take Case to the doctor, but I didn't want to. Taking him in would mean facing reality again, and I wasn't ready. So, I hugged Case tightly, stared into his beautiful brown eyes while wishing this wasn't happening, and put Case in his crib. I prayed he would sleep, before crawling into bed myself, hoping I could find sleep too.

My denial lasted less than twenty minutes. Case was whimpering and clearly uncomfortable. I could hear him from my bedroom. Sobbing uncontrollably, wiping snot from my face, I sat up. When I finally pulled myself together, I called Ryan and told him I needed to take Case into the doctor's office. The time had come. We needed to face this disease head on. I called Dr. Carina. The sleep study team had contacted her about how poorly it went, so her office told us to come in right away. They were ready for us.

We arrived at the clinic, checked in, and they immediately brought us back to a room, skipping the dreaded waiting room. Dr. Carina listened to Case's lungs and took a chest x-ray. She told me he had pneumonia and needed to be admitted to the hospital right away.

What? This is all happening so fast. I thought we were supposed to have more time before his inevitable decline.

Off we went. I drove to the hospital slowly and carefully, and followed their instructions to get admitted—frightened every step of the way. While driving, I called Ryan, who answered on the first try this time. I asked him to meet me at the hospital—maybe this sheer terror would be more bearable if I wasn't alone.

We got admitted, and things moved fast. They took another series of x-rays and put Case in a room. Then, they told us the pulmonologist was coming to talk to us. I hoped it was Dr. Michael.

They put us in a small, dark waiting room for parents. Despite the white walls and the bright midday light outside, the room was complete and total darkness. Ryan and I sat down on a green cot. It was the only splash of color in the room. The room, and our hearts, weighed heavy with darkness. Then, Dr. Michael walked in.

Thank God for a familiar face. But why is it so dark in here? It felt almost as if the lights, or lack thereof, were predicting Case's future—preparing us for death.

Can someone please turn the lights on?

Dr. Michael's presence was once again calming, though his news was anything but. "I know you were told Case has pneumonia. It's much worse than that. He has a collapsed lung. Unfortunately, it's time for you to make some of the tough choices we talked about last month."

He re-explained the three approaches to care with SMA: invasive, noninvasive, and palliative. An invasive approach meant using measures like a ventilator and possibly a tracheotomy. He explained that if we chose this route, he would recommend intubating Case, but there was a risk Case might never come off the ventilator.

Never come off the ventilator? Ever?

The noninvasive approach involved the use of a Bi-PAP machine, which would provide a continuous flow of air to his lungs to assist with his breathing. While it was designed to support his breathing, the doctors and nurses compared wearing the Bi-PAP to running a marathon every day. It was constant, exhausting work. This form of care could be life-saving for Case, and if we chose this route, it was less likely he would become dependent upon the machine 24/7.

Palliative care would focus on keeping Case comfortable, avoiding drastic life-saving measures. Although often associated with end-of-life discussions, Dr. Michael explained that palliative care focused on comfort and quality of life.

My heart was broken.

How? Why are we having these discussions?

Yet amid such sorrow, there was a wave of grace. Ryan and I had had a couple of months to research SMA care options, so we had already decided we didn't want to go the invasive route. For us, it came down to quality of life over quantity. Thank God we were on the same page. I imagine it would have been harder if we hadn't agreed.

That day, an odd thing happened to our relationship, as I am sure it does for many parents who have a terminally ill child. We transitioned from being life partners and friends to being business partners. We were in the business of life and death. A business we knew nothing about, and a business we didn't want to be in.

Dr. Michael gave us a few minutes to talk and checked in with us shortly after. When he returned, he brought his colleague, a Pediatric Intensive Care Unit (PICU) doctor. Case needed to be admitted to the PICU.

We informed them we wanted to go the noninvasive route, so their team prepared Case for this approach to care. The discussion was grave.

Then, they asked if we were religious, and if we had baptized Case.

We are, but we hadn't. Oh crap. Why are they saying this?

They got Case settled in his new room in the PICU and encouraged us to proceed with any religious practices we deemed appropriate because they weren't sure if Case would pull through.

Pull through? How? Already? We just found out he had SMA two months ago. This cannot be happening right now.

They weren't sure if Case would make it through the night. I was not ready for this.

When the PICU team was taking care of Case, I escaped to a computer down the hallway to update the CaringBridge site I had started for Case. It was time to have the prayer warriors storm the gates of heaven.

Looking back now, it's hard for me to read the CaringBridge journal. I was only twenty-three-years-old. How does someone who is so young put the dire state of their child's health into words? How does one request people to storm the gates of heaven on her son's behalf? It all felt heavy. Cruel. Detestable.

CHAPTER 6

THE ROLLERCOASTER

Case pulled through that night, and the next day, we brought our friends and family in to have him baptized. The team at the PICU was amazing to us. They had a strict two-visitor rule in the PICU, but they made exceptions in extenuating circumstances—such as when your child is likely to die before their second birthday, and it's uncertain whether he'll pull through the night.

Our pastor, Jude, brought the entire worship team with him for the baptism. I guess it's a good thing they made an exception to the rule because we were going to sneak them in. Our worship leader, Peter, played his guitar and sang.

Jude brought a beautiful brown bowl and a white handkerchief with a dove on it. Ryan and I stood beside Case, holding his hands while Jude baptized him.

"In the name of the Father, the Son, and the Holy Spirit."

There wasn't a dry eye in the room.

They hadn't quite figured out Case's Bi-PAP mask yet, so throughout the entire baptism, the tiny blue mask over his nose was ferociously leaking air into Case's eyes every time the pressure changed, making a whirring noise each time. We ignored it and savored the moment.

At the end of the impromptu but well put together baptism service, we all gathered around the small hospital room, stood in a circle, grabbed hands, and sang "I Can Only Imagine," by MercyMe. The PICU doctors and nurses joined us in the circle, holding back tears, and we lifted our voices in worship of God, hoping to intercede on Case's behalf. They all knew the end of Case's life was imminent, even though no one knew the exact day it would happen.

It was a weird feeling, knowing that death was looming. Yet, in that moment, there was an incredible amount of peace.

We all sang, many of us fighting through tears.

Singing was always, and always will be, the way I connect with God. The words of the song permeated my soul, worship embedded in my being—probably because I grew up going to church twice most Sundays, with my dad leading worship nearly every Sunday I can recall as a young child.

I wasn't the world's best singer, but I knew how to carry a tune, so music was my heart's song. Looking back, some of my favorite memories in that hospital room include moments of heartfelt worship—times where music carried me to another world. A world where my son wasn't dying. A world where there was hope. A world where I could simply be.

Case quickly developed a massive team of prayer warriors. The following on CaringBridge increased daily. It was the easiest way to get the message out to everyone quickly, so that I didn't have to tell the same story a hundred-plus times.

The day Case was baptized, my post read:

October 4, 2008

Cornelius was baptized today at 1:30. We were blessed with a wonderful time of worship with friends and family. Thank you to everyone who came. For those of you who didn't, it was beautiful. Not exactly the situation that you want your child to be in when they are baptized, but you could feel God's amazing, wonderful, and unconditional love in the room.

Please pray for a restful night for everyone in the family, especially Case. I posted a few pictures of the baptism so that we could share the special moment with all of you. Anyway ... More updates to come later.

The next few months were a rollercoaster. Many times, Ryan and I wrestled with the question: at what point are we playing God? Every decision felt like a desperate desire for control, a desperate attempt to change an inevitable future, a desire to hold on for one more day. How does one, at the mere age of twenty-three, make life-and-death decisions regularly?

My three sisters—Robyn, Dani, and Kelsey—had t-shirts designed. The front said, "Team Cornelius SMA Prayer Warrior," and Nahum 1:7 was on the back of the shirt, "The Lord is good, a refuge in times of trouble. He cares for those who trust in Him." Our community carried us through the highs and the lows.

On November 7, 2008, Case had a Nissen fundoplication surgery and a gastrojejunostomy tube (G-J tube) placed. Overwhelmed yet? I was too. A G-J tube is a long-term feeding tube placed into the stomach and small intestine. Aspiration from simple things like spit-up was a massive medical concern with SMA patients, so the G-J tube was placed to lessen the risk. Aspiration could lead to pneumonia, which could lead to a collapsed lung, which could lead to a breathing crisis, which could end his life, and, well, you get the point. We were hoping to avoid disaster.

Our friend Scott, the one who had helped me communicate Case's potential diagnosis to Ryan when he was home from his mission trip, threw an incredible benefit for our family. My brother-in-law Tanner cooked food for over two hundred people. Tanner is a professional chef, and his food was amazing, but on that day in particular, the rice turned into more of a mashed rice. He received more compliments about the mashed rice than any of the other incredible food he prepared. It was amazing, but we still heckle him about it today.

During the benefit, on November 15, our tribe raised $25,000. The local news station came out to the church where the event was held to highlight the benefit and encourage people to donate. We felt humbled and blessed. And, as an added highlight, Case was fresh out of the hospital, so he got to attend the benefit to see everyone who supported us.

I remember standing on stage and thanking everyone for being there. I was wearing a black dress and black tights—all black was a signature look for me. Ryan was in a suit with a blue button-up shirt. Adella was wearing a hot pink tracksuit, and Case matched her, but his was brown with an orange stripe.

Oh, how we hold onto these memories and pictures now.

Case's stint out of the hospital didn't last long, and we found ourselves in and out, in and out, in and out over the next few months.

When Case was home, I took on the role of a twenty-four-hour caretaker. He required breathing treatments every four hours around the clock. Each breathing treatment lasted about an hour, so by the time I finished, had sterilized the equipment for the next round, and checked Case's feeding tube, I had two to three hours before I had to do it all over again.

When I say around-the-clock, I mean around-the-clock. I had to do this overnight too. One at 8:00 p.m., one at midnight, one at 4:00 a.m., and then by 8:00 a.m. we were up for the day, starting all over again.

I was exhausted, so to promote sleep between treatments, I started taking Benadryl. If I took two Benadryl right before I started his treatment at midnight, I would be nice and sleepy by the time I was done and could sleep for two hours before waking up to start over again. Then, when I did the 4:00 a.m. treatment, I'd take two again so that I could sleep for a couple more hours before 8:00 a.m. hit.

I let Ryan sleep because he was still working and in school full time to become a teacher. I was on family medical leave (FMLA), and work was great about giving me time and space, but it was a huge financial constraint for our family. One of us had to work, and one of us had to take care of Case. That meant Ryan got to be the "fun" parent, and I had to be the detailed, structured parent making sure everything happened exactly when and how it was supposed to.

The hospital said it was normal for one parent to become the caretaker and one to have more fun with the family. I was a little jealous of Ryan's role—what I would give to be carefree—but I wasn't about to hand the well-being of my child over to anyone.

I was living on Benadryl and caffeine—consuming upwards of six-plus Mountain Dews per day. Looking back now, it's easy for me to see that was unhealthy, addictive behavior, but I was simply fighting to survive.

Having been through years of therapy and learned about the Polyvagal Theory, I now know that I was stuck in a constant sympathetic state of fight. I guess when your kid is fighting every day to stay alive, that's better than being stuck in flight, right? There was one thing I knew: if Case was going to fight, I was going to fight with him.

When Case was in the hospital—fifty-seven out of ninety days, to be exact—there were three PICU doctors that oversaw his care: Dr. Jed Sedgewell, Dr. Vic Studham, and Dr. Gigi Presly. Each doctor was on for a week, with a cover doctor coming in on Tuesday and Thursday evening so they could sleep. Honestly, they had to be exhausted, and we could typically tell. By the end of their week on, they admitted they needed a fresh set of eyes to look at Case's chest x-rays.

Dr. Gigi was definitely our favorite, Dr. Vic was hilarious, and Dr. Jed was a serious stickler. We didn't love him, but he knew what he was doing, so we let it slide and kept interaction to a minimum.

The first time I met Dr. Vic Studham, I leaned over and told Ryan, "Gosh, that's a porn star name if I've ever heard one."

The next day, when Dr. Vic entered the room, Ryan smirked as he said. "My wife thinks you have an exceptional porn star name."

My eyes nearly popped out of my face, and I leaned over, smacking Ryan on the arm. I felt mortified. Dr. Vic never let me forget.

During Case's hospital stays, the PICU became more than just a place of survival—it became a second home. The doctors, nurses, security guards, and hospital staff weren't just caregivers—they became our family. They saw us at our highest highs and our lowest lows. They celebrated the smallest victories, and held space for us when we were falling apart.

Hospital policy dictated a strict two-visitor rule, but the team, with knowing smiles and a few conveniently turned backs, rarely enforced it. I think they were more willing to turn a blind eye when the outlook was grim—not all kids face the same fate; not all kids face a death sentence. Friends and family filled Case's room.

Ryan and his friends often turned the tiny PICU room into a concert hall, hauling in their guitars and drums for impromptu jam sessions as security guards looked the other way. Laughter and music spilled into the hallways, a much needed sound when all you heard was beeping monitors daily. Music was always a part of us, and if Case was going to be in the hospital, then by God, the music was going to be with him. Nurses and other parents would often poke their heads in and smile. Even if only for a moment, the weight of impending death lifted. We weren't just a group of patients, parents, doctors, and nurses; we were a community.

Through those moments, we connected with other families facing their own battles—parents clinging to hope, children who had spent more days in hospital beds than playgrounds. There was an unspoken bond between us, a silent understanding that no one else in the world could fully grasp unless they had lived it too.

Ryan spent much of his time with his best friend Scott, visiting Case between classes on the days he didn't work while I tried to hold life together outside the hospital walls. As much as I wanted to be by Case's side every second, reality demanded otherwise. When your life stops, bills don't. They were piling up, and we were drowning in financial stress. So I worked one or two days a week whenever I could—because I had to.

At night, we switched. I'd rush to the hospital, ready to make up for lost time, while Ryan left for school or work. Our interactions were fleeting. We were ships passing in the night. We rarely saw each other, and when we did, our discussions centered around the business of life and death we were enveloped in. I didn't realize that maybe—just maybe—not seeing each other was a gift. It's easy to get along with someone you rarely see.

We had moments filled with laughter and moments filled with tears as we bounced in and out of the hospital.

While Case was in the hospital, we did everything we could to keep Adella's life as "normal" as possible. We had an amazing neighbor as our childcare provider, Jamie. Her son, Ethan, had passed away from cancer a few years back, so she knew the struggle of having a sick child. She was great, even taking Adella overnight on the nights when we had to stay at the hospital or make urgent medical decisions. Jamie became like a second mom to Adella—an imperative part of our tribe. I don't know where she is today, but if I could find her, I would say, "Thank you for showing us so much love, grace, and care during the most difficult time of our lives."

Once, when Case was at home—a rare occurrence—the physical therapist came over for a home session. I remember watching her set up and thinking, *What kind of therapy do you even do with a baby who will eventually lose all of his strength?* The thought made my stomach twist, but I pushed it down. I trusted the medical team, trusted the process, and let them lead.

Case lay on the floor beneath a brightly colored baby gym, soft toys dangling above him. The therapist gently positioned him, encouraging him with her bright, sing-song voice. I half-listened, sitting on the couch, my mind a swirl of emotions—doubt, exhaustion, the unrelenting ache of knowing what the future held.

Are the bills paid? Is Adella okay? Is Ryan okay? Can I do more to support Ryan's sobriety? Are there any appointments coming up that I'm forgetting about?

The therapist gasped. "Ashley, look." A smile spread across her face and her eyes widened with joy as her voice filled with excitement—something I hadn't heard in a while.

I turned my head and smiled.

My beautiful brown-eyed boy had his elbow completely off the ground, reaching up toward a toy.

He's never done that before.

A smile spread across my face and tears of joy filled my eyes.

He's trying. He's strong. He's still fighting.

For a moment, I allowed myself to feel hope. I continued to pray for a miracle harder than I ever had before.

———————————————

In December, we traveled to Salt Lake City, Utah, to see the top SMA specialist in the country, a doctor who was recommended by a parent whose daughter also had SMA. The goal was to learn more about how to care for Case and see if he qualified for a clinical trial. Since respiratory distress was a concern for Case, we couldn't fly, so we packed up our H3 Hummer—which now looked more like a makeshift ambulance—and made the twenty-four-hour drive to Utah.

Ryan's adventurous spirit meant he didn't let the fact that we were traveling in a makeshift ambulance with a child with a terminal disease keep us from seeing the sights or having fun. We visited the temple and the ski slopes, and on our way to the Utah Olympic Park, we encountered a man walking up the snow-covered road with his thumb out.

Ryan started pulling over the car.

"What are you doing?" I asked anxiously.

"Giving this guy a ride. He can't be going too far because we can only go up from here."

Oh, my gosh. He's crazy. First, a stranger is going to get into the car next to my son—who is wearing his Bi-PAP and has a feeding tube. And second, where is he going to sit?

I kept quiet as I listened to Ryan explain SMA and Case's situation to the perfect stranger.

I buried my head in Ryan's arm, mortified, letting Ryan explain the state of our vehicle, and another part was inexplicably jealous. How could he remain so calm in a situation like this? Even now, the memory still makes me smile. It's moments like this that I would never have the gumption to experience on my own.

Later that day, we made our way to Primary Children's Hospital to see the specialist. They ran a battery of tests on Case—a conglomerate of evaluations, including a DEXA bone density test—and even enrolled him in the current SMA clinical trial for valproic acid and spinal muscular atrophy. The team poked and prodded him relentlessly, asking every imaginable question about his health and his potential for life. I vividly remember Dr. Karen Sobella, kind yet direct, saying, "He's one of the strongest type 1 babies we have seen." Her colleague, Dr. Raya Mohn, nodded in agreement. Those words were the first glimmer of hope we'd had in a long time. Maybe his strength meant he'd live longer. Maybe we'd be lucky enough to see his second birthday.

The visit to Utah filled us with so much hope that we seriously considered uprooting our lives and moving to Salt Lake City to give Case the best care possible. While the PICU team at Centennial was incredible, many of the doctors were treating a child with SMA for the first time—they were alongside me and Ryan. It was frustrating to lead a team of practitioners, when we knew very little about the disease our son had and were learning on the go. But being in the presence of a doctor who seemed to know everything about SMA gave us an incredible amount of confidence and hope.

Amidst the mortgage crisis of 2008, short-sales were all the rage in Utah, and I spent every spare moment scouring listings for the perfect handicap-accessible home. Inevitably, Case would be in a wheelchair, so handicap-accessible was at the top of my list. The prospect of a fresh start in a place where top-notch care was within reach was the most hope we'd felt in a long time. And Utah wasn't so bad.

As the year drew to a close, we clung to hope and prayed that we might finally spend Christmas together. We knew we only had a few Christmases to celebrate, and we certainly didn't want to celebrate in the walls of the hospital. We hoped to join Ryan's family in Harrison Bay State Park for the holidays. The incredible team at Centennial Children's Hospital poured their hearts into making our dream a reality, as long as Case's health allowed.

CHAPTER 7

THE CHRISTMAS GIFT

On December 23, 2008, the team at Centennial told us they were going to discharge Case so we could spend Christmas in the Harrison Bay State Park with Ryan's family. We felt thrilled. It was the best Christmas gift ever.

Case had a special car seat called a car bed. It was a small yellow and red box that looked a bit more like a coffin than a car seat, but it's what we had to use to safely and legally drive with him in the car. So we loaded the vehicle with his car bed, suction, oxygen, and cough assist. Once again, it looked more like an ambulance than a car, but we were ready. Ryan pulled up to the valet entrance, and the medical team helped us out to the car with Case. When we got to the lobby, the child life team was waiting with three black garbage bags filled with Christmas gifts from the hospital for Adella and Case.

Tears filled my eyes. We were so loved.

When we arrived at the ranch owned by Ryan's parents, I immediately went to work setting up Case's space. The shelves in the walk-in closet were perfect for housing all of his life-saving machines. It took about an hour to get settled in; then it was time for his respiratory therapy.

On Christmas Eve, we opened the gifts from the hospital. We had more books, dolls, teething rings, and sensory toys than we knew what to do with. Case and Adella both squealed with excitement and joy. Adella danced around her brother, singing with joy until she passed out on the couch with rosy red cheeks. To this day, those squeals of sheer joy were some of the happiest moments of my life.

The second night we were there, Case's oxygen kept dipping into the eighties. With SMA, you get concerned anytime it goes below ninety-six because of how quickly SMA patients can decline. I chalked the dipping oxygen levels up to needing a new pulse ox for his big toe. Residue on the reader led me to believe it wasn't functioning correctly—at least that's the story I was telling myself. Looking back, I know I was in denial. I wanted a normal Christmas. I wanted a normal life.

On December 26, 2008, Ryan wanted to take me snowmobiling in Gatlinburg. My mother-in-law, Kathy, was going to take care of Adella and Case so we could have some fun. We hadn't had a normal day without machines, routines, fear, or worry since October second. Deep down, I think Kathy was terrified. My mom and Kathy were both trained to care for Case, but it was a significant responsibility accompanied by a magnitude of stress.

We took off in the morning, despite Case's oxygen continuing to dip. Kathy made us write on a napkin who our children would go to if we died before we left. We said our friends, Josh and Katie. They were amazing. If anything happened, hopefully our napkin-will would suffice.

When we got to Gatlinburg and unloaded the snowmobile, it was freezing. It had to have been below zero, but dammit, we were going to have fun. Heated handlebars on the snowmobile were a lifesaver. I'd reach around Ryan just to grab the handlebars to keep my hands warm. It felt good to be close, to not have the worry of the world between us.

As we were riding through a valley, Ryan went up a massive hill. I clenched my fists and grabbed onto Ryan as hard as I could, hanging on for dear life. "This is a terrible idea." In my mind, it looked more like a cliff than a hill.

Partway up the hill, the front end of the snowmobile went into the air, and we flipped head over tail end. Ryan bailed immediately, and I followed shortly after. I rolled about 15 feet down the hill and stopped because my head hit a tree.

Okay. I'm alive. It's okay. Dang, that could have been bad. Turns out Kathy's instinct was right, having us write who our kids would go to. That was a close call.

"Why did you do that?" I gave Ryan a nasty look. He stood up, laughing hysterically, and told me to calm down.

(Side note: Men, these aren't words you should use with your already disgruntled wife.)

The snowmobile was upside down in about two feet of snow. It took both of us using all of our might to get it turned over, but we got it.

Ryan put the key in the ignition and turned it. Nothing happened.

It was freezing, and the temperatures were getting colder. The increasing wind had me convinced we were stranded and would die in the hills—cold and alone.

Okay, okay, I may be a little over-dramatic.

We tried several times, and the result was the same—still nothing. Ryan believed the engine had flooded from going head over tail.

No shit, Sherlock. I was having fun, but now I'm pissed, and I just want to go home.

Finally, we heard snowmobiles in the distance. They were coming our way, thank God. Three good Samaritan snowmobilers stopped and helped us wipe off the spark plugs so we could get the snowmobile started again.

We played around for a couple more hours before loading everything up and heading back home to see how Case and Adella were doing. It was a good day.

Greeted by Kathy as we stepped into the house, she said, "I don't think he's okay. I don't think it's his pulse ox; I think he's having a hard time breathing."

I did a breathing treatment, said a prayer, and we went to bed. The next morning, we headed home. That Christmas, we made so many memories and had so much fun. Looking back, those were once again memories that I would hold on to forever.

By that time, we had finally gotten home health nursing approved, so anytime we were not in the hospital, we had a nurse who would come and take care of Case during working hours. This allowed me to go to work and make a little money, thus relieving some of our financial stress.

The nurse that was on the next day when I went to work was very new and had never cared for an SMA patient. Her name was Bonnie. I was extremely nervous leaving Case in her care, but I was a rule follower, and the rules of our in-home nursing contract said they would only be there if Ryan and I were not home. Weird, I know, but those were the rules.

At 3:00 p.m., I received a concerned phone call from my brother-in-law, Tanner. He lived with us and had just gotten home. "Ashley, Case's oxygen is eighty-two. I sent the nurse home. She didn't know what she was doing. You need to come home."

My denial was hardcore, so rather than calling the doctor and having her do a direct admission to the PICU, I brought him to the emergency room.

When we arrived at the emergency room, the doctor who was seeing us didn't even know what SMA was.

Are you kidding me?

When he stepped out, I called the PICU team and asked them to come downstairs and get us. It was against the rules, but they did it anyway.

That evening, Dr. Jed was on. Ryan, worn very thin, asked Dr. Jed if he thought it might be time for us to let Case go.

What? You're there already? No, absolutely not. Not now. Not yet.

Dr. Jed assured us that at some point, SMA would end Case's life, but he didn't think it would happen this winter. He thought we might have the conversation next year when the flu season hit, but not this year.

Whew.

He encouraged Ryan and me to go home and spend some time telling each other how we both felt. "Even if you go to bed on a different page, at least you know what page the other person is on." He also told us that parents with terminally ill children often get divorced.

Thanks, dude. Helpful.

We went home and had a conversation. Ryan was ready to let go, and I wasn't—especially after our conversation with Dr. Jed. We knew we couldn't decide until we were both on the same page.

A few days passed, filled with difficulties, strong emotions, and highs and lows. By now, we had a consistent stream of visitors on a fairly regular basis, so people were constantly coming and going to keep us company and wish us well.

On January 5, Ryan wasn't feeling well at all. He had a horrible sinus infection, so he went home to sleep. My friend Jillian came to the hospital to keep me—and Case—company. At one point when she was holding him, Case looked into my eyes, and as I looked into his beautiful brown eyes, all I could hear ringing in my head was, "Mommy, it's okay. Mommy, it's okay."

Eventually, I joined Ryan at home to sleep. The hospital regularly encouraged us to sleep at home so that we could get as much rest as possible and keep some sense of normalcy in our lives.

As I took my Benadryl and fought to find sleep, I couldn't get the look of Case's eyes out of my head. They looked so sad and so tired.

The denial hit hard.

CHAPTER 8

THE GOODBYE

On January 6, we were excited to go to the hospital. Dr. Gigi was on duty with a fresh set of eyes, and we knew she would cut the crap and tell us how Case was really doing.

She did, and the news wasn't good. "I'm concerned about Case's x-rays. I've been monitoring his progress from home, and he's getting worse," she said. Once again, we discussed how we would know it was time to withdraw care. She assured us that Case would lead the way and let us know when he was ready.

He will tell us when he's ready—"Mommy, it's okay. Mommy, it's okay." Case, is that what you meant?

My mom came to the hospital that day, and she, Ryan, and I went down to the cafeteria for lunch. They were serving nachos, and I had a massive plate. I mean, it's hospital cafeteria food, so what would you expect? I topped my nachos with pickled jalapeños and stared down at them in disgust.

Ryan and my mom were discussing what Dr. Gigi had said and how we'd know when it was time. I may have been part of the conversation, but there was a dialogue going on in my head that I couldn't ignore.

"Mommy, it's okay. Mommy, it's okay." Oh my goodness. *Why? Why did you have to tell me that the night before? Dr. Gigi told me you would tell us when it's time. Why? I'm not ready. I can't do this.*

No. No. I won't. I can't.

As my mom and Ryan sat talking, I slammed my hands down on the table and said, "Enough already. It's time. We know it's time. He doesn't want to fight anymore."

My mom looked at me and confidently said, "Okay. Let's go upstairs and talk to Dr. Gigi." I think with the tone in my voice, she could tell I had already spent plenty of time mentally agonizing over the decision, and it was apparent Ryan had been ready since December 28—the entire duration of this hospital stay. It took me from December 28, 2008, to January 6, 2009, to get there. Ten agonizing days. A pace that may seem rapid, but for SMA patients and families, quick change is all too common. Things can literally change in the blink of an eye.

We spoke with Dr. Gigi and told her we were ready to withdraw care from Case and switch to comfort care. We discussed what that meant. She promised us three things: "He will never be in pain, he will never be alone, and he will never be afraid."

The cool part about withdrawing care or moving to comfort care, if there is a cool part, is that his hospital room felt more like a home. We moved out all the equipment and machinery, only keeping Case connected to oxygen to keep him comfortable. His BiPAP, cough assist, and suction were gone. We also moved in an enormous bed for the family so that we could all spend time with Case. Dr. Gigi told us it could be hours, days, or even weeks. Committed to making whatever time we had left the best, we enjoyed our time.

That evening, our Life Group from The Refuge came to the hospital to worship with us and pray over us in a semi-private waiting room. Mid-worship, someone knocked on the door. It was my mom.

"Ashley, you need to get out here." She sounded frantic.

I walked outside the waiting room where we had been worshiping. There were over fifty people lining the halls.

"Who are all these people?" I asked.

"I'm not sure, but they are all here to see your beautiful baby boy because his story has impacted them so strongly."

I don't remember all the faces, but I remember many of them. If you came to see Case and I never thanked you, thank you. The kind words, love, support, and hugs we received warmed our hearts. Our church and the people surrounding us sure knew how to be the hands and feet of Jesus.

Since Case had a G-J tube, the only food he had eaten throughout his entire life was breastmilk. And you don't really eat that. So, we decided it was time for him to try his first food—a banana. As ten-plus people stood around and watched, we let Case eat a banana.

The banana had a few brown spots on it, which meant it was extra sweet. The second the banana hit Case's tongue, he let out a happy squeal. His arms reached toward the banana, his eyes saying, "More please." He panted excitedly. It was almost as though he was trying to talk, but simply couldn't get the words out. He loved it. My heart was overjoyed, yet fear loomed. I'm so glad he got that banana, but looking back, we really should have given him some ice cream.

We made it through the first night, and Case was still holding on strong. In fact, his oxygen levels increased at one point, causing me to second-guess our decision and want to scream for the doctors and nurses to implement all life-saving care.

The medical team said Case's final days would be a rollercoaster, filled with highs and lows. They let us know that at some point we would question our decision and want to recant; we'd freak out mentally and want to do anything and everything we could to save our baby. I resisted the urge to ask for life-saving measures because they had told me this would happen.

The next day, I updated CaringBridge. The post read:

January 7, 2009

The unknown still lurks around our room. We have no clue how long Case has left with us, and that is the hardest part. Case is doing surprisingly well. He had a great night of sleep. It still amazes me how a little boy completely dependent upon machines to live can do so well after having been off of them for just about twenty-four hours. His strength keeps me going. We are on Case and ultimately God's time right now.

Please pray for peace and comfort. The days that are to come are going to be very difficult. For the past three months, my entire life has been based around this child. My eating, my sleeping, my going about and doing things, everything has depended on him. There will be a huge sense of relief when Case passes, but I also think I might feel a little lost. This is my life, Case is my life. I know that with my strength and faith in God, I will make it without him, and I will see him again.

We are enjoying this time, as long as it may be. For the first time in three months, we can hold our little man while he is sleeping free from any machines. It is a huge blessing to have and make these memories. Also, please pray for Ryan as his sinus infection is making him pretty miserable. I cannot imagine going through all of this and feeling sick on top of it.

It is our faith that has brought us this far.

That evening, several members of our church and our family came to worship with us again. They had Case on alternating doses of morphine and Ativan to keep him comfortable. I sat in a rocking chair with Case. He was just wearing a diaper. It seemed like the perfect way for a baby to be—practically naked.

My mom looked over at me and both of my legs were shaking vigorously. I was rocking back and forth, holding Case, staring blankly ahead, numb to the fact that anyone was in the room with us—mentally freaking out.

"Do you want us to sing?" someone asked.

"Yes," I snapped.

"What do you want us to sing?"

"I don't know. Just sing." I rocked back and forth as my knee bounced up and down.

They sang song after song.

My mom snuck out the door and grabbed Dr. Gigi.

"Oh no, is Case okay?" asked Dr. Gigi.

"It's Ashley," said my mom. "She's panicking."

Gigi was the best. She came in, knelt down, put one hand on my knee and one hand on Case's arm. "We can give him more morphine or Ativan anytime you ask Ashley. And if you'd like,

I can call your doctor and see if we can get you something to help you calm down and get some sleep tonight."

"Ok, give him more medicine, please. And I'm fine with you calling my doctor too." He had been crying and wincing, and I was so mad because Dr. Gigi promised me he wouldn't be in pain. Whether physical or emotional, the end of life is painful no matter what.

At some point, we wrapped up worship, and it was just our family left in the room. We sent Adella home to sleep with Ryan's parents.

Before attempting to fall asleep, I remember staring fervently into Case's eyes. Dr. Gigi had explained that at some point, Case's oxygen level would get so low that he would fall asleep and never wake up again. I stared into his eyes and didn't want to fall asleep because I was worried I might never see his beautiful eyes again. Tonight, they looked sad. Ready.

I attempted to sleep in the bed with Case all night. He vomited twice during the night, so neither of us slept much. If I drifted off for a second, every time I woke up, I would glance up and to the left to see the monitor and read his oxygen levels. He was still hanging out in the eighties. Gosh, this kid was a fighter.

The next morning, the CaringBridge post read:

January 8, 2009

It feels as though the decline of Case's body has begun. Last night there was about an hour where he was very irritated and very restless, but we had our church and friends here to literally sing us through it. We got him all the meds that he needed, and he has been resting peacefully ever since. His heart rate is going up and his oxygen is going down. It could be a slow and steady decline, or it could be slow and then suddenly happen. We do not know. The one thing that we know is that our little guy is going to be in heaven rejoicing with the Lord soon.

We had a Now I Lay Me Down To Sleep photographer come in and take pictures of our family. Case was doing well when this happened, so it was a fun moment for our family. We made hand prints of our entire family, hand prints for just Case, and footprints for just Case. We also got clay necklaces with our thumbprint and Case's thumbprint in them. The hospital has been amazing getting us everything we need and getting all the things that really need to get done, done for us. A huge thank you to Centennial. We really feel like part of your family, and because of our little Case, we always will.

I am going to hold my baby boy. Hold him, hug him, and love on him. That is what he needs, and that is what I need. We love you all, thanks for praying!

That day, since it was a workday, our visitors mainly comprised family and a few of Ryan's friends from the twelve-step program. Around 10:30 a.m., Dr. Gigi and Carla, the nurse, encouraged me to take a nap. I once again locked eyes with Case, but I knew I needed sleep. I made Ryan and Scott promise to wake me up if anything changed.

I woke up shortly after noon. Ryan and his friends were still in the room, along with my mom and sisters, Dani and Kelsey. Case's oxygen was only fifty-six.

Oh my goodness. Fifty-six. That's almost halfway to zero. It's happening. I'm not ready for this. I can't do this. Please God, please. Heal my baby.

I freaked out. How could everyone be in the room singing and having fun? How did no one realize his oxygen was only fifty-six? The nurse came in and turned off the monitor.

"It'll be better for you if you don't know, Ashley. Trust me. Spend time with your son. Don't worry about his oxygen. When it's time, he'll go," the nurse said in a calming tone.

Around 1:00 p.m., Dr. Gigi came into the room, looked at me and Ryan, and said, "It's time." We had asked to be notified when the time was near so that Ryan and I could be alone with Case.

It's time?

What does that mean? Minutes? Hours? How much time is time?

God, save my baby.

Actually God, take him and make it fast and peaceful.

No, don't. Help.

I can't do this.

No. No. No!

How am I supposed to do this?

We asked my mom to stay in the room with us. Everyone else went to the waiting room down the hall. I had my freak-out moment the night before and internally earlier that day, and this was Ryan's freak-out moment. He was a new Christian, and he was unprepared for the death of our son.

"Can you read the Bible?" he said to my mom, panic filling his voice.

"What do you want me to read?" she asked.

"Read. Just read." Ryan said, as his grip on my hand tightened.

So my mom opened her Bible and began reading from verses she had underlined. Eventually, she landed on Romans 8:38–39.

"For I am convinced that neither death nor life, neither angels nor demons, neither the present nor the future, nor any powers, neither height nor depth, nor anything else in all creation, will be able to separate us from the love of God that is in Christ Jesus our Lord."

Neither death nor life. Nothing, nothing, nothing can separate us from the love of God. Nothing. Not even death.

Ryan and I had both crawled into the small bed with Case. Ryan was sitting on Case's left side and I was on his right side, snuggled together like a happy little family. We listened to my mom read and loved on Case.

Then, Dr. Gigi walked into the room and asked my mom to leave because the time was drawing near. My mom left the room, and Gigi and Carla both looked at us and said, "It won't be long now. If you need anything, or if you get scared, push the button, and we'll come right in."

No, God. No.

We had Life 96.5 turned on the radio, and the song "Fly to Jesus and Live" came on. For twenty-three minutes, we sang to Case through laughter and tears. It was some of the worst singing I've ever heard, but it didn't matter.

When my kids were in the baby stage, I always sang "You Are My Sunshine" by Jimmie Davis and Charles Mitchell to them. On this day in particular, Ryan and I changed up the words to the last two lines.

You can take
Our sunshine away

After singing a few times, Ryan and I looked at each other and at Case. Miraculously, he opened his eyes for a split second. I leaned forward to take the sight in one last time, "Ryan, his eyes. He opened his eyes." And just like that, he closed his eyes and exhaled deeply.

We sang a few more songs and cried a few more tears.

I leaned forward to look at Case more closely. "Is it over?" I asked.

Just before 2:00 p.m., we pushed the call button.

It took Dr. Gigi and Carla forever to come into the room. I later found out that it was because they were all standing around watching the monitor, sobbing. Ryan and I anxiously discussed how awkward the whole thing had been, not hearing a breath, thinking it was over, then suddenly he'd breathe again. When they finally came in, they talked to us for a little while and asked us how things had gone. After a couple of minutes, Dr. Gigi took her stethoscope, listened to Case's heart, looked at Carla, and said, "2:02 p.m."

January 8, 2009

Cornelius John passed away this afternoon at 2:02 p.m. Ryan and I got to lie in the bed with him, hold him, and sing him to Jesus.

I will post details about family visitation and the celebration of Case's life later. We know our baby is in heaven, SMA-free, walking and running with Jesus.

Ryan and I looked at each other and asked, "What now?" We invited our friends and family into the room because Case looked so peaceful.

Carla went to the nurses' station to grab some warm blankets. Dr. Gigi went to the room to let the family know that Case had passed, and that we were ready for them to come and say goodbye to him. "Deb, Dani, Scott, Tanner, and Adam, you can go into the room now," she said.

My fifteen-year-old sister Kelsey looked at Dr. Gigi and asked, "What about me?"

"I'm so sorry. Ryan and Ashley didn't say your name."

Dr. Gigi frantically followed the group to the room, peeked her head in the door, and asked, "Was there a reason you wanted Kelsey to stay in the waiting room?"

"No. No, please go get her," we said. She ran to the waiting room to get Kelsey, who sat on a couch by herself with her head in her hands, sobbing.

To this day, we still laugh about the fact that we forgot to say Kelsey's name. We could cry about it, but we choose to laugh instead. As a fifteen-year-old, I'm sure it was pretty traumatizing for her. But the funnier part was when my mom told us later that she looked back at Kelsey and thought, "Well, I'm not sure why you can't go in, but I'm going. See ya."

We called Ryan's parents and asked if they would bring Adella and Tanner's daughter, Jessica, up to the room. Since we were cremating Case, this would be their last opportunity to see their brother and cousin. Kathy wasn't sure about the decision, but we assured her that Case looked very peaceful and "less scary" than when connected to his machines.

When Adella walked into the room, I sat in a blue rocking chair holding Case. She walked up to the chair slowly, touched her brother's hair, and looked up at me and said, "He's so white. He's beautiful." She hardly knew her colors.

For about an hour, we played guitar, let people hold Case, and loved on our little boy.

Then the moment came. "Ashley, the funeral home is here whenever you're ready."

Ready? To take my boy away? No, I'm not ready. How does one get ready for this moment?

It was early January in Nashville, Tennessee, and colder than normal, so it was freezing outside. The hospital team let us know that they never let their kids leave the hospital alone, so Dr. Gigi bundled up in her black parka with brown fur around the hood and grabbed some warm blankets.

"Ashley, whenever you're ready," she said again.

I gently placed Case in her arms, and we wrapped the warm blankets around him. "He won't be alone," she said.

As she walked out the door, I peeked my head out of the room and looked to the right to see an image I will never forget. Dr. Gigi walked down the hallway with my son, escorted by two men in black suits from the funeral home who looked a bit like bodyguards. An image that still haunts me, yet carries so much love and kindness.

I wanted to follow them down to the hospital lobby, but I couldn't bear the thought of seeing my son put into a hearse.

I looked to the left to see the nurses' station.

What am I supposed to do now? Every other time we said goodbye, it was a see you later, not goodbye. This time, it's goodbye. We'll never be up in the PICU again. This is weird. What am I supposed to do? I'm leaving without my boy. This isn't how I wanted this to go.

Lord, help me. Give me the strength to carry on.

PART 2

THE AFTERMATH

2009 – 2013

CHAPTER 9

THE CELEBRATION OF LIFE

How does one continue moving on after such a life-shattering event, especially at twenty-three, when still a child myself? My life had revolved around Case; but it's odd, I didn't realize how much until I started writing this book.

He had become my everything.

And then, one day, he was gone.

A piece of me was gone with him. I remained forever changed. Case taught me to be a fighter. When you see your son sitting in a hospital, helpless, unable to speak for himself, you go to every measure to fight for him. No one else is going to do it, so as a mother, you have to. Don't get me wrong, Ryan was great at helping us fight, but there is a weight that a mother carries that no one else can.

Now that Case's fight was over, I didn't know what to do.

Looking back, I feel a tremendous amount of guilt about how little time I gave to Adella during that period in our life because everything revolved around Case. I was doing the best I could and trying to survive—young kids, a newly sober husband, and bills to pay. Adella, if you're reading this, please know how much I love you.

We planned a Celebration of Life for Case at 2:02 p.m. on Saturday, January 10, 2009, exactly two days after his passing. There were two funeral homes in town that provided complimentary basic services for children under the age of eighteen. We selected Spring Hill Funeral Home.

When we arrived the day before the funeral, we sat downstairs at a large boardroom table with Pastor Jude, Pastor Peter, and the funeral directors, and we planned the celebration of life for Cornelius John. Jude and Peter were great; they came with a ton of suggestions on Bible verses and songs. It all felt surreal, almost as though I was dreaming a horrible dream and would wake up at any moment.

But it was all very real.

While meeting at the funeral home, there was a point where Ryan and I were alone in the boardroom. A floor-to-ceiling curtain covered one wall. I leaned over to Ryan and asked, "What do you think is behind the curtain?"

Of course, in true Ryan fashion, he unabashedly walked over to the curtain, yanked it, and pulled it back. Lining the wall were the tiniest baby caskets imaginable. My heart sank. A lump welled up in my throat. Tears filled my eyes.

Thank God Case is getting cremated. I could never put anyone through seeing my beautiful baby boy in a tiny casket like that.

Genesis 3:19 says, "For dust you are and to dust you will return." Ryan felt strongly about ashes to ashes and dust to dust. And while it was a conversation I never thought I would have that young, there I was. First, I made life-and-death decisions, and now I was making afterlife decisions.

How fun.

When we wrapped up the service details, we asked the funeral directors when they would cremate Case. We wanted my sister Robyn—who was flying in from California—to see him before cremation. Since we weren't having him embalmed, strict timelines dictated that cremation must proceed quickly. They assured us that if Robyn arrived by the next day, she could see him. We planned on returning the following day with Robyn, so she could say goodbye.

Later that day, as I sat at my dining room table surrounded by the paperwork that made up the cold business side of death—a side few people ever discuss—my phone rang. The call was from Primary Children's Hospital in Utah.

"Hello?" I answered.

"Ashley, it's Dr. Raya. We are so sorry to hear the news of Case's passing. Our entire team is shocked. He was the strongest type 1 SMA baby we have ever seen, so we didn't even get the chance to discuss what happens in the clinical trial if a participant passes away. We'd like to fly a doctor from Johns Hopkins to Nashville via private jet to perform an autopsy on Case. This would require sending his body from the funeral home back to the hospital. Is that okay with you?" Dr. Raya explained.

I hesitated only for a moment before replying, "As long as we can still proceed with cremation, I'm fine with it."

I couldn't help but think—*didn't they mention the clinical trial details? I'm glad they left out the morbid specifics; I doubt we'd have clung to hope if we'd heard about the dying part.*

Later, we learned that the team at Centennial Children's never allows their pediatric patients to be alone in the morgue. So, Dr. Gigi met the Johns Hopkins doctor in the hospital morgue—a perfect display of the care and commitment she always showed. They wrapped up the autopsy and brought his body back to Spring Hill Funeral Home.

The next day, when Robyn arrived, she was extremely hesitant about seeing Case. Ryan and I both encouraged her, insisting that his calm, peaceful appearance—devoid of the tubes and machines—would facilitate healing. We believed that saying goodbye at the funeral home might help ease the pain.

She agreed, hesitantly.

My dad, Ryan, Robyn, and I walked into the funeral home. It was a frigid day, one that almost seemed to take the air from your lungs. The funeral director greeted us with a warm smile and calming presence. "We have Cornelius wrapped in some blankets on a small table in the viewing room on the left," the funeral director said. "You may enter whenever you're ready."

I knew this would be the last time that I would see my baby boy's body. I knew in spirit he wasn't here, but this was still a big moment. And I wasn't sure I was ready for it.

Robyn and I decided we would enter the room together and spend some time alone with Case. Robyn walked through the door first, with me following closely behind.

Case was sitting on a table about twenty feet in front of us, in a room far too big for the intimate moment we were about to experience. I recognized the hospital blankets wrapped around him as his body lay on the table near the front of the room. Blankets I had come to love over the course of the last three months. He looked like he was sleeping—so peaceful and so calm.

As soon as Robyn saw him, she turned around as though she was going to flee the room to escape the pain, a look of sheer terror and panic on her face. She started sobbing and dropped to the ground, every bit of air taken from her lungs.

I caught her as she headed toward the floor, grabbed her, and wrapped my arms around her, her head on my chest, saying, "It's okay, Robyn, it's okay. He's with Jesus now. It's okay." Every word coming out of my mouth was one that I desperately needed to believe.

At that moment, I knew what she was going through. I knew how shocking it was to see such a beautiful boy, once filled with so much life, so many tiny giggles and laughs, and so many smirks and smiles—to see him lifeless and pale, lying on a table in a funeral home. A repugnant yet beautiful sight.

It is a moment and a feeling I will never forget—seeing the heartbreak on my sister's face and being the one to comfort her. Even as I write this today, over sixteen years later, I sob reflecting on this moment. We've spoken about it a few times since, and she always tells me how backward that moment was, that she should have been the one consoling me, not the other way around. But all things work exactly as they should, and in that moment, I needed to be the one comforting my sister. I needed reassurance that I was okay, that my world hadn't ended, that I could still be kind and caring to other people. I needed to know all the things that felt so untrue. Comforting other people gave me a purpose, a reason to live.

Eventually, we walked to the front of the room and Robyn held Cornelius John while we talked about how peaceful he looked. I rubbed his head, feeling that his once soft spot was now sunken in completely—apparently that happens when life no longer flows through one's body. Aside from that, he looked perfect. After a while, my dad and Ryan joined us in the room. We shared some of our favorite memories, cried a few tears, laughed a few laughs, and then we left.

I don't remember walking away from Case's body. It's puzzling which memories stick with me as though they were yesterday and which ones I can't recall.

The next day, we held Case's Celebration of Life. Five of our favorite nurses from the PICU attended, all wearing their signature navy blue scrubs. It made our hearts so happy to know that our little guy had impacted the nurses in such a profound way—a sign his life and death both mattered.

At the start of the service, we walked down together as a family and extended family. Kelsey walked with Adella and Jessica and snuck out to bring them to the nursery after the procession. We all wanted to pay attention, and that's hard to do when you have a two-year-old and three-year-old talking to you constantly or relentlessly asking why everyone was crying and when they could see baby Case.

As Kelsey was walking back from the nursery, she saw Dr. Gigi, arriving late because she had come from the hospital. "Come with me," Kelsey said. "Come sit with our family."

"I can't do that," Dr. Gigi responded softly and kindly.

"Ryan and Ashley would want you to sit with the family. Come with me."

Having just left the hospital, she was wearing her navy blue scrubs. As usual, her long black hair slicked back in a ponytail like it almost always was. She snuck in with Kelsey and sat in the row directly behind us. I saw her and sobbed—tears of happiness and joy. She was and always will be our favorite doctor.

The service started with praise and worship, singing "Blessed Be Your Name," by Matt Redman. The lyrics talk about how the Lord gives us life, but then he also takes it away, yet we continue to bless His name. It felt like an odd song to sing, yet perfect at the same time. I absolutely lost it when we got to the bridge, but I continued singing through the snotty hysterical crying, raising my hands to the Lord.

We also sang the song "Shadowfeet," by Brooke Fraser. My favorite singer from the church band, Katie, wasn't available that day, but Peter and the team put the song to a different key and figured it out just for me. Just for Case. The chorus explains that when the world crumbles, we can remain strong through God; even when everything is gone, we can still stand with Him.

The world had most definitely fallen out from under me, and the only way I was still standing was because of God, the amazing community of people surrounding me, and a fair share of adrenaline—from which I was soon to come crashing down in an absolutely unforgettable way.

After the service, Ryan and I stood in the back of the sanctuary, greeting people as they entered the fellowship hall for a meal and a time of love and laughter. At one point, I leaned over and said to Ryan, "Who are these people?"

"I don't know," he said. We looked at each other, smiled, and continued shaking hands and hugging people as they passed by. We felt a tremendous amount of love. These were the people who had carried us through.

Looking back now, I wish we had gotten pictures of everyone who attended. I wish we had recorded the message Pastor Jude gave. I remember very little of it, but I remember him saying, "I'm jealous of Cornelius. I'm a pastor, and I've spent the better portion of my adult life trying to lead people to Christ and encourage a community of believers. And this little boy, who never spoke a word in his life, did that better than I ever did and with only his eyes."

I remember thinking that was such a unique perspective. And that day, those were words I needed to hear. It was Jude's first funeral for a baby—maybe even his first funeral ever. He did a great job. His words gave purpose to my boy's life, and they gave purpose to his death—something we so desperately needed to hold on to.

CHAPTER 10

THE REPRIEVE

I can't explain the tremendous amount of relief I felt after Case's passing. It's a beautiful thing not having to spend every waking moment worrying it might be your son's last. It is astonishing how both relief and sorrow can coexist.

My brother-in-law, Matt, had joined my sister Robyn in Tennessee in time for Case's Celebration of Life. He stayed a couple of days to spend time with Ryan and me, making sure we were okay.

Oddly enough, those few days following the Celebration of Life were some of the happiest days I remember having in my entire life. We didn't have a plan or a schedule. There wasn't anything we had to do. We could simply have fun and do what we wanted when we wanted.

We went bowling. Matt and Robyn shared a pitcher of beer while we bowled, laughed, and forgot about life for a while. It certainly didn't feel like we had just lost our son. For the first time in a while, it felt like we were living. You see, when your life revolves around a terminally ill child, it consumes every morsel of your being. Instead of being a normal parent, going on playdates and worrying about whether they'll learn how to tie their shoes, every waking moment is consumed by rigorous schedules, treatments, and appointments. Your life revolves around keeping your child alive. It was exhausting, so to live without constant worry, in a way, it felt like freedom—freedom that coexisted with the deepest sorrow one can imagine. In all of our pain and agony, we were relieved to feel that peace.

When we got home, we played endless battles of *Guitar Hero*. We took turns playing guitar and singing, having the time of our lives. If someone drove by our house and looked through our window, they'd never know we'd just lost a child. We laughed until we had tears in our eyes and played until we were so tired we could hardly keep them open.

Then, it was time for Matt to leave, and my brain started to panic. My hands were clammy, my heart raced, my chest tightened, and I couldn't think straight. His leaving signified the closing of one chapter and the beginning of the next. It was a chapter I wasn't ready to close, and definitely one I wasn't ready to begin—the beginning of a life without Case.

God knew we needed a little more time. Matt's flight was canceled because of the cold temperatures. I can still see the image of Matt walking back into our house after returning from the airport. He was a man of large stature, and our side door was smaller than your average size door. Matt had to duck to get into the kitchen. I'd never felt so happy to see such a tall man walk into my kitchen.

"Well, do you want to play another round of *Guitar Hero*?" He said.

Oh boy, do I want to play another round of Guitar Hero?

We played late into the night, allowing the game to captivate our minds, providing a temporary escape from the reality we were living in and the grief we were so desperately trying to escape. Deep down inside, I knew it was going to come to an end, so the entire evening I felt a knot in my chest. Moving on and beginning the next chapter was inevitable.

And, as they say, all good things must end. The next day, Matt's time with us ended. It hit me like a freight train. Matt going back to California meant other people were carrying on with their lives.

How can people keep going on as though nothing happened, when my world feels like it has come to a complete halt?

I felt frozen, like a movie scene where everyone else was speeding by, but I was standing still. I wanted to scream, "Stop! Stop! Everyone, my baby died. Can you just stop for one moment?"

But, life continues. It's the hardest part of grief to explain to those who haven't experienced it. Life goes on, even if you can't.

And, go on it did—rapidly—a pace I was awfully familiar with.

Two weeks after Case passed away, I went back to work. I remember little of that time, but I do remember people staring at me like I had three heads—turning away, not knowing what to say, awkwardly avoiding me. I felt alone. I felt like I would never be the same again.

When I returned to work, my mom came over with a friend to clean our house while I was gone. The seemingly mundane tasks of life—like wiping down counters, folding laundry, and vacuuming—had become insurmountable in my world consumed with grief. It was hard enough getting out of bed and going to work. Cleaning? No, thank you.

That evening, after work, I did what I always did. I walked into Case's room, ready to spend time in the black La-Z-Boy rocking chair. It was my safe place, the one place where I could let my tears flow freely. I could let my guard down and pretend, if only for a moment, that he was still with me. I opened the door to his closet, and my hands reached into his laundry basket, ready to grab some of his dirty clothes so I could smell my boy one more time. The scent brought him closer to me.

I bent down, ready to pull out a pair of his adorable footed pajamas to my face, breathe him in, and rock in the black La-Z-Boy rocking chair while singing lullabies that used to reach his ears.

His laundry basket was empty.

His clothes were gone.

I couldn't comprehend what was taking place. Panic set in—I dropped to my knees, gasped for air, and sobbed uncontrollably. I couldn't breathe. I felt like I was dying. I felt broken. Hopeless.

Earlier that day, my mom had washed all of his laundry and donated his clothes and toys to Goodwill. I knew she was donating his clothes. She had asked if it was okay. But I hadn't thought to say, *Hey, leave the dirty laundry, Mom. I need his smell to survive.* I didn't realize that the clothes in that basket were my last tangible connection to him. They were the last pieces I could hold, feel, touch, and smell. Every night, his smell had been my lifeline as though it alone was carrying me from one day to the next. And now, with one load of laundry, it was gone. The only thing left I could hope to glean a scent from was Case's fox tail. Because he had little strength, sensory toys were his favorite, and for some odd reason a fox tail was what he had clung to during life. But the foxtail hardly held his scent.

I knew my mom meant to help, and I couldn't bring myself to tell her. I was too heartbroken to form the words, too devastated to explain how her kindness had shattered my heart in ways I didn't think were possible.

One wash cycle. One load of laundry. And now all I had were memories and pictures. His smell was gone forever, and I felt like I was drowning. The ocean of life was going to take me under.

Several days later, Ryan and I loaded Adella into the car and headed to church, forcing ourselves to do one of the normal things we had done before Case's passing. The Refuge had become our safe place, somewhere we could exist without fear of judgment, where we could breathe—if only for a little while. It was a strange feeling, though. Everyone knew who we were. We had been on the prayer list for over five months, our names spoken from the stage nearly every Sunday evening, our journey followed closely by those who had never even met us. In a way, we had become whatever the church version of a celebrity is— recognizable, prayed for, whispered about—even so, among the many faces, there were plenty of names I didn't know.

I loved being there, and I dreaded it.

The church was young, vibrant, and growing, which meant there were always pregnancy and birth announcements. Each Sunday, another couple stood on stage, smiling from ear to ear as they shared their news. The congregation would congratulate them with cheers and applause.

This Sunday, we were in for yet another birth announcement. A couple that Ryan and I knew well had just welcomed a healthy baby boy. Pastor Jude shared the news with excitement. As he made the announcement, joy filled the room. People were cheering, clapping, and celebrating the gift of new life.

How can you cheer and be so happy? Don't you know my son died? Doesn't anyone recognize this? Can't anyone see how badly I am hurting?

Their happiness felt like a brick on my chest. I wanted to run, to scream, to remind everyone that while they were celebrating life, I was still mourning death. I missed my son. I wanted to hold him in my arms. Their happiness was too much for me to handle.

But I smiled and clapped along with everyone else, forcing my hands to move. I even whispered a quiet, "Congratulations," to the couple when I passed them after the service. They looked at Ryan and me with overwhelmed eyes, unsure of what to say.

Externally, I remained composed. Internally, I was unraveling. I was dying slowly, being carried out to sea by a tide of grief I hadn't seen coming—one that was filled with other people's children. Yet we continued attending The Refuge. Every time Pastor Jude announced a birth or a pregnancy, I held my breath and pretended everything was okay. I acted as though my world hadn't fallen apart. Our church was young, and the announcements were frequent. Each time, the words felt like a fresh wound, a harsh reminder of what I had lost. I hated feeling that way, but grief has a way of twisting even the happiest of circumstances into cruel reminders of what we've lost.

Several months after Case passed, a couple about our age had a little boy named Sam. He had blondish-reddish hair and big blue eyes that spoke volumes, just like Case's brown eyes had.

One Sunday, Ryan leaned over and whispered, "Do you think they'd mind if I held him?"

I paused for a second to think, but before I could say anything, Ryan had already asked. They smiled and handed Sam over without question.

Ryan took him into his arms, lifted him up, and smiled looking directly into his eyes. He rocked him gently as the worship music played and the congregation around us sang. He swayed, singing softly, completely lost in the moment. For the first time in weeks, Ryan looked like he was happy. He needed this. I knew he did.

But for me, it was difficult to watch.

Tears filled my eyes as I watched Ryan hold a child that wasn't ours—a beautiful boy with a beautiful family—something we were supposed to have.

That's supposed to be our son you're holding. God, why did you take my boy away? Why?

Inside, I was broken. Watching Ryan hold Sam was unbearable. An insurmountable wave of grief came crashing over me. My arms and heart had never felt so empty. Yet, as much as it hurt me, I knew Ryan needed this. I knew it was his way of coping with the grief. We both had our own ways of handling the loss of our son. Maybe Ryan holding Sam was no different from me sitting in that black La-Z-Boy rocking chair singing to a boy who was no longer here. No two people grieve alike, and this was how Ryan survived. He held Sam, swayed, and smiled, even though he wasn't our son.

Every Sunday, we sat in the same spot. And many Sundays, Ryan would hold Sam, singing and dancing through worship, smiling as if for just a moment the world was okay. And I would sit beside him, longing for it to be my son in his arms, missing Case so deeply it felt like I might shatter, all the while a smile on my face.

Week after week, I sat in church, with everyone around me celebrating life while I was grieving death. Each week I hoped eventually I wouldn't have to pretend anymore. My world was spinning, and I wanted it to stop.

CHAPTER 11

THE VERTIGO

About a month after Case died, I started experiencing dizziness like I had never before. It literally felt like the world was spinning.

I know the world is actually spinning, but I'm pretty sure I'm not supposed to feel it.

It got so bad that it began interfering with work and everyday life. I was a banker at the time, and I would sit at my desk with a customer in front of me when a bout of vertigo would hit. Suddenly, I would be gripping my desk for dear life, unable to concentrate, and the customer would look at me and say, "Are you okay?"

I'd respond, "I'm fine, just a little dizzy, that's all. I'm sorry."

As soon as the customer left, I would make my way to the couch in the break room, lay down, and close my eyes until the vertigo passed.

The times I spent playing with Adella became fewer and farther between, leaving Ryan to once again be the fun dad while I retreated and tried to keep my world from spinning (faster than it was supposed to). Not only had I lost my son, in a way, I'd lost my daughter too.

This led me to my family doctor, who sent me to a specialist, who sent me to another specialist, and so on—until I had seen fourteen different doctors. I still remember the appointment that gave me the most hope.

I was sitting in the exam room at the neurologist's office. The doctor was an older man with gray Einstein-like hair and hunched shoulders. He walked into the room, looked up from his clipboard, shook my hand and said, "I think I know what's wrong with you."

Finally. Relief is in sight. There is hope.

"It has nothing to do with why you're dizzy," he added.

What the heck? Then why even say that? Totally, completely, utterly unhelpful.

He explained he thought I had Raynaud's disease, which had nothing to do with the dizziness but everything to do with why my hands felt so cold when he shook them. So, I proceeded with the test for Raynaud's, which involved submerging my hands and feet in ice-cold water, then measuring my blood pressure in each finger and toe.

The testing room was dark, more like a torture chamber than a medical facility.

Why aren't the lights on? This is weird. What in the heck are they about to do to me?

They brought in a big vat of ice water, taped devices to my fingers and toes, and asked me to put my hands in the water. Though it felt like my hands were submerged for ten minutes, the research I've done for this chapter shows cold stimulation tests usually only last twenty to thirty seconds. It's strange how the brain distorts memories.

After submerging my hands, we repeated the process with my feet. And all this effort didn't even address why I was dizzy. It felt odd, but I went along with it anyway.

It hurt. I'm not a fan of the ice baths that are all the rage today, so this test was definitely not for me. In the end, hundreds of dollars and an ice bath later, I found out I didn't have Raynaud's. Helpful—not.

I had CT scans, MRIs, nerve conduction tests, and countless other procedures. Every doctor gave me the same response: "Your baby just died. You're stressed. Stress is causing your vertigo." I wasn't happy with that answer. There had to be a better reason.

After seeing specialist after specialist, I turned to the only thing I knew: prayer. Ryan and I were part of a Life Group at church, and every Tuesday night, they'd ask for prayer requests. Every Tuesday, I'd ask them to pray for me, and they would. One girl in the group, Melissa, kept mentioning her chiropractor and how he might help.

Finally, after weeks of praying, Melissa came up to me and said, "I made you an appointment with my chiropractor on Thursday. I know he can help you."

What else could I do but go?

When I went to the chiropractor, I found out that I had a massive amount of pressure on my vagus nerve. This nerve plays a key role in maintaining balance in the body. The specialists weren't all wrong. The chiropractor said it is possible the extreme stress I had experienced during Case's life and death caused the pressure.

Stemming from the fact that my neck had lost its natural curve, the doctor knew he could help. I started receiving corrective chiropractic care. Right away, the dizziness intensified as though the merry-go-round was suddenly being pushed by the biggest, fastest boys on the playground and they were hoping to make me cry and get me sick. The doctor stated it was a healing crisis, or a temporary increase in symptoms, and for the first time in a long time, the brain and body could communicate better than before.

Although skeptical, I continued with the care plan. What other option did I have?

After one month of corrective adjustments, my body healed, and my vertigo dissipated completely. I was able to play with Adella again, have fun with Ryan, and perform at work. I felt like I had my life back. But Case still wasn't there. Even though he wasn't there, I found something I was excited about—health and wellness. My health transformation was so powerful that it ignited a passion in me for chiropractic and overall well-being. Having finally found something I was passionate about, I left my job and started working for the doctor. My life had a renewed sense of purpose. Besides being an employee, I could finally be a mom, a wife, a sister, and a friend again. Living life, once again.

One day, shortly after starting my new job, my phone rang. I glanced down at my phone. It was someone from church. I answered, expecting a friendly, "How are you doing?" or maybe someone looking for me to swap nursery duty with them.

"Ashley, I wanted to reach out to invite you to a grief support group at church," she said.

Awe, how nice of them to think of me. Although, a grief support group? A bunch of sad people sitting in a circle, crying together? No, thank you. Not my jam.

I had barely processed my grief. Why would I willingly step into a room filled with more of it? It sounded daunting, never-ending, and horrible.

"It's primarily a group of women who have had miscarriages," she continued.

Suddenly, I felt lightheaded and dizzy, as though the vertigo had returned. My vision blurred. Disbelief filled my mind.

Miscarriages? Are you freaking kidding me? My heart pounded in my chest. *I held my baby, changed his diapers, kissed his cheeks, and smelled his perfect baby smell. And now he's gone.*

A part of me wanted to lash out, to scream that this wasn't the same. How could they compare my loss to theirs? I had lived ten months and ten days with Case in my arms, and now I had to live the rest of my life without him. They never even got to hold their babies.

And then, like a Mack truck, God hit me with a moment of clarity.

Ashley, that's precisely why they are grieving. You got to have and hold your baby. They never got to live those experiences.

The dizziness subsided, and something in me shifted.

Grief wasn't a competition. Loss was loss, no matter the form. Pain doesn't come with a ranking system. In that moment, my perspective on grief changed forever. And I found some grace through it all.

"I appreciate the invitation. But I'm not sure that's for me. Should I change my mind in the future, I'll reach out." I politely replied, grateful God had spared me the pain I would have induced on another human being had the thoughts in my mind come out of my mouth unfiltered.

CHAPTER 12

THE PARDON

While I was enjoying my new job, Ryan was attending Belmont University to become a teacher. We rarely saw each other. I worked during the day and two nights a week, while he worked during the day and attended classes at night and sometimes vice versa. To be honest, it completely stressed me out, but probably not for the reason you'd think.

Ryan had a criminal record—a felony drug charge—that would prevent him from teaching. Yet, his unshakable, unwavering faith kept him marching on. He was certain that God would allow him to teach, so he went through two years of education and six months of student teaching on the belief that God would make a way. Maybe that statement alone shows his faith was indeed stronger than mine.

Looking back, I'm not sure if it was faith, confidence, belief that the rules didn't apply to him, or a combination of all three, but he was definitely persistent.

He petitioned the Governor of Tennessee, Harrison Blackthorne, for a pardon. If you've never been through the process (and I hope you never have to), it's rigorous. He had to publish a notice in the newspaper, collect letters of recommendation, and find people willing to testify before the Tennessee Parole Board on his behalf.

Ryan was a salesman, so he made all of this look remarkably easy. The chiropractor I worked for hit it off with Ryan from the very beginning, so he was a shoo-in to testify for him. Testimony from prominent individuals in the community boded well for those seeking executive clemency. Ryan also got our pastor, Case's doctor, our worship leader, his twelve-step program sponsor (a well-known businessman), most of his college professors, and several other prestigious members of the community to write letters of support. The letters he collected along with pictures of his journey filled a three-inch, three-ring binder.

He submitted everything. Then he presented his case to the Tennessee Parole Board, with over seventy people showing up to support him, the largest showing they had ever seen. And after receiving a unanimous recommendation to Governor Harrison Blackthorne on behalf of the Tennessee Parole Board, we waited. Ryan's letter to the Governor read:

The Honorable Harrison Blackthorne

November 11, 2009

Office of the Governor

600 Dr. M.L.K. Jr Blvd

Nashville, TN 37243

Dear Governor Blackthorne:

My name is Ryan Antony, and I write to humbly ask for executive clemency. My life up to this point has been one of painful yet intense learning experiences. My life has also become full of joy and the spirit of God. The most important experiences in my life have transformed and shaped who I am today. My story is common to most alcoholic/drug addicts in the sense that I was raised with a good family in a healthy environment. In high school, I experimented with alcohol and drugs, which led me to do things outside the morals and values that my beautiful parents had raised me with. My history with alcohol is riddled with selfish, self-centered, and destructive activities. For more than ten years, I was on a destructive path, ruining everything I touched. I hurt people everywhere I went, and I had fallen completely off the path of righteousness. Believe me when I tell you that I was unworthy of the freedoms granted to me by my country and fellow man.

I am not the man I was when I was convicted of possession of a controlled substance. Incarcerated for the second time, exhausting opportunity after opportunity to straighten out my life, I began reading a series of spiritual books in prison. There I began my spiritual journey, which continues today. My spiritual beginning in prison was not a burning bush experience, but rather an awakening to the idea that there was a God and that He was not me. I began to grapple with the idea that He created me and this world; that He loved me and was not a vengeful and wrathful God that I had misunderstood Him to be in my childhood.

In prison, I realized I must stay sober and finish college. In 2005, I was on parole living in a hotel, serving tables full time, attending Nashville State Community College full time, and completing a year long meth program. I was focused on school more than anything: achieving academic honors that earned me scholarships to Belmont University. I completed the meth program and was recommended by my parole officer for an early release from parole. During this year, I met my future wife Ashley, who became pregnant with our daughter Adella. Previously, the only times I had been sober were the times I had been incarcerated.

Ashley was raised by an extremely devout Christian family in Bowling Green, Kentucky. She knew God had a bigger plan than I could see. Racing to get my life in order for marriage, I bought a duplex house and worked two jobs. My daughter was born and we got married. We rented the other half of our duplex and I started school in Belmont while working only one job. By summer, Ashley was pregnant again. That point was the beginning of the most beautiful life I could have ever imagined possible.

I took that year away from school and became heavily involved in a twelve-step recovery program, focusing on my spiritual journey. I went to a meeting every day, and started working with my sponsor, doing the steps, and taking an inventory on my life. I had been told the promises of the program, and I knew it was my only hope for permanent sobriety. I was making a solid foundation built with the principles and traditions of the twelve-step program; God was the mortar cementing these building blocks firmly in my life. Ashley and I attend The Refuge, where we are supported by a community of sober people who are believers of Christ. On February 28, 2008, my son, Cornelius John was born and my life seemed complete; we were the perfect American family. The Refuge took me on my first mission trip teaching Latino orphans in Los Angeles about Christ. I took on service positions in the twelve-step program, and became the chairman of the board of the Southside group, which is the largest in Tennessee. Truly I was doing what God intended me to do in my life.

On July 28, 2008, Cornelius (Case) was diagnosed with Spinal Muscular Atrophy. The doctor told us that Case would die within two years. Our life consisted of long hospital stays, and painful realizations that our son was going to die. On January 8, 2009, Ashley and I held Cornelius as he gasped for his last breath, singing to him his favorite song, "You Are My Sunshine." There were over fifty people in the halls of the hospital waiting to hold our son, and pray over his body. I had never felt and saw love like I saw that day. Case was ten months ten days old and had brought together an entire community of people. His life strengthened everybody it touched. His story is a legacy that is my responsibility to carry on. My life now has purpose. Ashley and I speak at events and tell our son's story. We are actively involved in Children's Miracle Network to help them raise money during their telethons. I speak at treatment centers and at recovery meetings. I travel with a Christian band and tell my story. I attend meetings and help suffering alcoholics by relating our pain and struggles that are universal. I attend Belmont University because I want to teach high school kids Literature. I have a double major in literature and secondary education. Most importantly, I have a true relationship with my parents, wife, child, brother, family, and friends. No matter what is going on in my life I teach Adella about Christ, we sit down as a family and eat supper everyday, I read her to sleep every night, and I keep the spirit alive in my daughter through the memory of her brother Cornelius.

My future is bright. I am a weekly patient at my chiropractor's office, which has helped heal my back problems. I am currently working at CIGNA Teldrug as a salesman and have been employed with them for two and a half years. I have been the top sales representative for six months of the last year. Although this job is temporary, I am making the best of it while I am here. My real passion is to teach adolescents and help them grow through the study of literature. I have been called to share life through literature with high school students. When I was in high school, I didn't have positive role model teachers that truly reached out to me when they knew things were going badly. My unique story allows me to empathize with students in high-risk situations. I have the ability to relate to people who are suffering and who are lost. Through my story of drug/alcohol use, imprisonment, freedom, schooling and every life experience in between, I can effectively help high school students work through their problems and make decisions for positive solutions. I have worked tirelessly to achieve a 3.4 GPA at Belmont University. You must realize that teachers have always told me I would never achieve success in school because of my attention-deficit disorder and dyslexia. Reading literature is an essential part of life, and it has been overlooked and pushed aside by television. I have been blessed with an outgoing, upbeat personality that will draw students into reading. Through reading, I will help students empathize with characters and relate to their personal stories in class. There is an infinite amount of knowledge passed from student to student when guided properly, and I plan to facilitate learning that will last a lifetime. Adolescents are our future. I will produce the future of America with critical thinking young adults with tools to sustain and maintain meaningful lives.

I approach a crossroads in my academic career. Next year I need to student teach in order to graduate college. With a felony on my record, I will not be able to student teach. Without the student teaching, I will not be able to graduate college with my secondary education major. Also, I need to be able to take the teacher certification test, but with a felony record, the state school board will not allow me to take the test. These are major barriers to my goals.

Governor Blackthorne, I am asking for a pardon because I desire freedom from the bondage of my past. I want to take my daughter to Canada where we have family. I want to travel to other countries and go on missions to witness for Christ. I want to be able to enter prisons and witness to men who are lost and dying on the inside. I want to be able to teach children literature. I am not the Ryan I was. I am a permanently transformed man.

I will never take for granted the decision you have to make. I need you to know that whatever the decision, I will serve God without regrets. A pardon opens doors that are currently shut. Without a pardon, I will continue to pour my efforts into the doors that remain open. Thank you for your time and consideration of this request for executive clemency. I pray for your administration, that you are blessed and that our state is blessed and protected by you.

Sincerely,

Ryan Antony

A noteworthy letter, remarkably written. The wait ensued.

Then on December 6, 2009, Ryan and I went out for sushi at our favorite restaurant in town, Blue Sushi Sake Grill, to celebrate his birthday. We were not well off, so dinner out was a special occasion.

Blue Sushi Sake Grill was a hole-in-the-wall restaurant, where each booth had its own private cove. When you walked in, you immediately knew that the sushi was amazing or totally sketchy—there's no in-between. I met Ryan at the restaurant right after work. As soon as the host seated us, Ryan had a look on his face—an excited, happy, just can't wait kind of look. His smile spread from ear to ear and his eyes lit up brighter than the

Christmas lights outside. He reached into his bag, pulled out an envelope, and held it up across the table so I could see what it said. "The Office of Governor Harrison Blackthorne."

This has to simply say they've received his request. There's no way he's already decided and replied. Oh gosh, do we want to ruin a good night? My birthday is already ruined. Why ruin Ryan's too?

I looked at him, wondering if he really wanted to open it right then and there. Of course he did. He was supposed to begin student teaching in a few weeks, and a pardon would eliminate a huge hurdle that his professors had already helped him overcome—finding a school that would allow him to student teach with his colorful background.

"I'm opening it," he said, pulling the envelope toward him and ripping it open.

Taking the letter out carefully yet forcefully, he stared at it for about ten seconds before screaming, "I knew it! Best birthday present ever," and threw the letter at me so I could read it.

A smile spread across my face. God had opened doors we thought were closed. Being granted a pardon on his birthday was the best gift of all, just twenty-five short days from the time the Parole Board recommended him and he submitted his letter. It was a gift from God—a wave of grace.

Coincidentally, it was the same day that Ryan had been arrested for his original crime. Everything seemed to have come full circle. The timing was fitting. With his pardon, the future held endless possibilities. My worries were finally at ease. Everything was going to be okay. God had a plan, and it was bigger and better than mine.

While completing his student teaching during the winter of 2010, he applied for a position as an English Teacher at the high school where he had been a student teacher. After interviewing, he received a job offer. It was the news we had waited such a long time to hear, and we were excited beyond belief. Ryan and I could both do something we were passionate about in the community we loved. Life started falling into place.

But during the background check process, human resources said that his history did not align with the values and beliefs of the school. They didn't tell us what they found in his background, but it was devastating and confusing news considering his recent pardon. Ryan valued honesty and shared his background while student teaching before receiving his pardon. But once human resources found out, they rescinded the offer.

To make matters worse, they informed him he could never get a teaching position in the school district—the largest district in our area. It seemed so incredibly unfair that a man could put in all that time, energy, and effort, get pardoned, change his life completely, and still have his past held against him.

"What now?" I said.

"I'll find something else, God has a plan. I'll keep applying, and I won't stop until I get something. Eventually, I'll find a teaching job. Everything will be okay, Ashley." He was confident, as always, and certain things would fall into place. Either that, or he was delusional.

"Where will you look?"

"I'll try Chattanooga. It's a great city, and my family is there. And until something falls into place. We'll stay here."

"Okay," I said, feeling let down by the news.

Two steps forward, one step back.

CHAPTER 13

THE ADOPTION

While we were waiting for Ryan to find a teaching job, we discussed growing our family. After Case's SMA diagnosis, we met with a genetic counselor at Centennial Hospital, who informed us that both Ryan and I carried the gene for spinal muscular atrophy, which meant getting pregnant carried severe risks.

Being an autosomal recessive disease, if we were to conceive, there was a 25 percent chance the child would have SMA, a 50 percent chance they would be a carrier but not have SMA, and a 25 percent chance they would not carry the gene at all. The odds were not in our favor, and I certainly didn't want to go through that experience again. It was a decision only we could make with guidance and information from our genetic counselor. A decision that is much easier to make when both partners are on the same page. We weren't.

Ryan thought it was worth the risk of having another baby, but I wasn't on board. Looking back, it made sense— our experiences of loss were vastly different. I had been Case's primary caretaker and nurse. I took care of every feeding, every breathing treatment, every machine, and every doctor's appointment. Ryan was the provider and the "fun dad." He carried a different weight—one of financial and emotional support, but he didn't experience the daily time-consuming tasks and routines that had kept our son alive.

The idea of starting over and willingly stepping back into the role of full-time medical mom seemed crazy. After Case had passed, I was relieved to hang up that hat and move back into being just mom. Putting the hat back on wasn't something I could fathom doing. The thought alone crippled me. Ryan, on the other hand, didn't feel the same anxiety. We discussed having more kids, disagreed, and let it sit for a couple of months.

At one point, we tossed around the idea of adoption, but even that led to disagreement. Where I saw an opportunity to care for a child without reliving the trauma of loss, Ryan saw us raising someone else's child. He wanted *our* child, not someone else's. So we reached an impasse and agreed to disagree.

Then, one day, in typical Ryan fashion, he came home from work with a grin beaming from ear to ear and exclaimed, "Ashley. I made an appointment with an adoption attorney tomorrow. We need to get our fingerprints and our background checks completed tomorrow."

"What?" I cocked my head to the side, placing my hand on my chin.

"Tomorrow. We'll go in tomorrow. The attorney is in the same building as your office. It's perfect." He spoke fast, and continued to smile as he paced back and forth across the kitchen.

"Tomorrow? Adoption?"

"Yes, that's what you wanted, and I'm finally there. Let's adopt a baby." He extended both arms and came in for a hug.

I was ecstatic, yet in complete shock. Overnight, he had changed his mind. *Where did this come from? I thought we would never agree on a path forward to grow our family.*

I knew very little about the adoption process, especially with an adoption attorney instead of an agency, but we jumped in headfirst. From what little I knew, it could take twelve to twenty-four months and it could be an arduous process. While we were waiting for our background check to come back, our attorney began showing our adoption profile to potential birth mothers, something that made my stomach churn considering Ryan's past.

Don't get too far ahead of yourself. Ryan has an extremely colorful past. I hope it doesn't keep us from adopting.

But quickly, our background checks cleared. I felt like I could breathe again. Step one, complete. The same day, we received our first potential match with a birthmother. But when it came time for her to make the final decision, she selected another family. It turns out adoption carries a significant risk of loss too—the risk just looks different. No matter how hard we tried, we couldn't get away from heartbreak completely.

The chiropractor I worked for was in the same building as the adoption attorney, which made communication very convenient. One day, while the office was very busy, the attorney's wife (who was also his assistant) came sprinting down the stairs, knocking frantically on the door. When I opened it, I could see the excitement on her face. With eyes wide and bright and a broad grin across her face, she announced, "You've matched with a birth mother."

Six months into the process, we matched with a birth mother—a timeline I could hardly believe. Like most things in our life, adoption was full throttle. It happened fast, and it was completely overwhelming.

Am I ready? What if I lose another child? Can we do this? Thoughts filled my mind.

A young college student from Texas had chosen Ryan and me to be her child's parents.

Gosh. How does someone make that decision?

It was exciting and a tremendous amount of pressure to succeed at the same time. Being a parent is a lot of pressure. Being selected by someone else to parent their child for life is excruciating, scary, an honor, and a joy—all at the same time. Because everything happened so quickly, we had little time to think about it. We simply moved forward, trusting God every step of the way.

The adoption journey was an emotional rollercoaster for our family, as I am sure it is for many. In many ways, it was more unpredictable than having a terminally ill child—a journey filled with heartbreak and hope. Twice before the baby was born, the birth mother changed her mind and decided to keep the baby. Each time, the news felt like a knife to my heart. Each time, I relived the loss of Case. Each time, the dreams we built around that child came crashing down in an instant.

Yet, despite the pain, we didn't give up hope. We couldn't.

Before being induced, the birth mom once again changed her mind. This time she agreed to place her son for adoption. When the attorney broke the news to us, I was filled with relief, joy, and an aching sadness. It was a combination of feelings I had never before experienced. I continued to hold my breath as though waiting for the other shoe to drop. When you've been let down enough times, you start to think hope is gone for good.

Driving to Texas was nerve-wracking, knowing all the while that the birth mother could change her mind at any moment. She had up to five days after the birth of the baby to change her mind—talk about anxiety. *What if I fall in love with this baby and she changes her mind? How will I handle the heartbreak of losing yet another child after holding him in my arms?*

The minutes went on like hours, the hours like days.

In typical fashion for us, we encountered a series of challenges on the way—*three* flat tires. You can't make this stuff up. The tires on the vehicle we had purchased only had a 25,000 mile warranty, unbeknownst to us. While driving to Texas, we hit 35,000 miles, and one by one, the tires decided they had seen their last days. Each time, we pulled over on the side of the road, unloaded our tiny white Nissan Versa hatchback packed to the brim with a pack-n-play, diaper bag, loads of diapers, and all the baby gear you can imagine. Ryan would put on the spare tire, and we'd head to the closest auto shop.

Thank God, each time we found an open tire store or someone willing to stay past their normal hours to help—a benefit of being married to a salesman. We told our story as they swapped out the tires. Each time, they wished us the best of luck, and we took off. We had given ourselves ample time to get to Texas for the scheduled induction. Thank goodness because we needed it.

When we finally arrived, we checked into the hospital. Because the birth mother didn't want to meet us, the hospital team put us in a different section of the hospital and essentially told us not to leave the room without an escort. We were in a large oddly shaped room without windows. It was well lit, but the lack of windows left me feeling claustrophobic.

Maybe it's the anxiety?

The medical team informed us when she was getting close to delivering the baby, and they immediately came to the room when the baby was born, excited to announce that our son was healthy and well. We had signed all the paperwork ahead of time so that as soon as he was born, they could bring him to our room. When they told us he was born, it took ninety minutes for them to bring him to us. It was excruciating.

"Oh my gosh, what is taking so long?" I said anxiously.

Ryan smiled as he continued pacing back and forth. "I'm sure everything is fine."

"Do you think she changed her mind?" I anxiously swayed from side to side with my hands on my hips.

"No. Stop worrying," Ryan said as he continued to pace.

"What if she changed her mind? What if we came this far just to lose another baby? I can't handle that again. What will we tell people?"

"Ashley, it will not happen. Everything is fine."

Ryan's positive attitude persevered and my anxiety played worst-case scenario. It turned out that it was shift change, and they had lost the paperwork during the handoff from the day crew to the night crew. They needed to find the paperwork before they could bring our baby boy to us. Each second that passed left me worried the birth mom had changed her mind. It was horrible. It didn't help that the last time we entered a hospital, we left without our son.

After ninety agonizing minutes, the nurse finally rolled a bassinet into our room. She glanced down at the bassinet with a grin on her face, looked up and said, "Ryan and Ashley, meet your son."

For a moment, I couldn't breathe. When I regained my senses, I stood up. My heart was pounding. I peered into the bassinet. Then, I looked up at the nurse and asked, "Is this the right baby?" The words came out before I could stop them.

He wore a striped pink-and-blue knit cap, his head covered to keep warm. His skin appeared far lighter than that of his birth parents, and I hadn't learned that black babies are often born a few shades lighter, with their melanin deepening as time passed. I gently removed his cap and all uncertainty disappeared as curly black hair popped out from underneath.

The moment I saw his hair, I knew. He was ours.

And just like that, I was in love. I'm not a fairytale love sort of person, so I don't believe in love at first sight when it comes to romance, but love at first sight with adoption is 100 percent real. He was ours, and he was perfect.

I picked him up. Had Ryan let me, I would have held him for fourteen days straight. I was his, and he was mine. My heart felt full again. We named him Azariah Cornelius. Azariah means, "he whom the Lord has helped," and Cornelius means, "horn of war," obviously a name picked after his brother. Something to carry his legacy into the future, and a fitting name.

While we were in Texas, we stayed at the local Ronald McDonald House. While it was a huge financial blessing, it wasn't the most comfortable place to be with a newborn baby in tow. Our room held a small window unit air conditioner that hummed, whistled, and ticked like a clock every time it turned on. When we stepped outside, the scorching July heat felt heavy. But this didn't stop us from making the most of our time. Ryan was an adventurous spirit, and he couldn't sit still, so he made sure we were occupied from morning to night.

Because I didn't give birth, I had energy. I could walk, run, skip, and enjoy all the experiences with my newborn baby and husband. So, we did all the fun things.

We visited the local Coca-Cola Museum. The air-conditioning was a welcome relief from the relentless humidity outside. Everywhere we went, we took pictures. We wanted to savor every moment and capture memories to share when we were home.

We wandered through a city park. I wore Azariah in the Moby; I loved baby wearing. Plus, it was great for bonding with our newly adopted child. The parks in Texas were beautiful. Trees were covered with Spanish moss. Beautiful pink and purple flowers filled the air with an incredible scent. We took in every scent and moment.

We even braved a swamp tour with a newborn baby in tow. I held a washcloth in my hand, and poured cold water over it regularly, touching it to Azariah's forehead and chest so that he wouldn't overheat. During the swamp tour, we got to hold a baby alligator, feed marshmallows to a raccoon, and hope our finger didn't get bitten off like the tour guide's did. No joke. There was no strict schedule, no routine, nowhere to be, so we just enjoyed it and had the time of our life.

In the evenings, when the heat began to dissipate, we retreated into the cool temperatures of the local movie theater. Azariah slept soundly through every movie we watched. Our window unit air conditioner had a hard time keeping up with the Texas humidity, so we spent very little time at the Ronald McDonald House.

Finally, life felt normal. Throughout the trip, I held onto hope that everything would continue that way after we were home.

Five days after Azariah was born, our attorney called to let us know the birth mother had voluntarily terminated her parental rights and a judge had signed off on the paperwork. A wave of conflicting emotions washed over us—immediate relief and heartbreak. We were relieved the birth mom could no longer change her mind, that the fear of losing him had finally passed. But we ached for her and the loss that she had experienced.

I imagined what she must have been feeling at that very moment—wondering if she had made the right decision, if she would ever stop grieving the child she had carried and loved. I thought about the emptiness she might have felt walking out of the hospital without him, her arms aching in a way mine once had when I left the hospital without Case. I held a lot of empathy for the emotions she may have carried.

Adoption is beautiful, and it is born out of loss. And in that moment, as much as we celebrated, we also mourned—for her and for the pieces of her heart that would always belong to the little boy who was now sleeping soundly in my arms.

After seventeen days, we received approval through the Interstate Compact on the Placement of Children (ICPC), allowing us to cross state lines and go home. We couldn't wait for Adella to meet her new baby brother.

CHAPTER 14

THE MOVES

Life took another unexpected turn during the summer of 2011. Ryan received a job offer for a teaching position in Chattanooga, Tennessee which was near his family. The opportunity offered a sense of familiarity as we established our new normal, and we decided it was something we couldn't pass up. The thought of having his family close to us to enjoy Adella and Azariah while helping us navigate our grief seemed to take a weight off of our shoulders.

Yet, with every new beginning, there was a weight of uncertainty. I worried constantly. As a child, my nickname was "Worry Wart," and it seemed to follow me into adulthood. I feared the further we got from our incredible community, the more we'd fall apart. Could we continue healing there? Would Ryan stay sober without his twelve-step home group? Would we find a new church? Could we carve out a life of peace and grace there? Despite our doubts, we packed up our tiny world and set our sights on Chattanooga, clinging to hope for the future with all the strength we had, and a five-year-old and one-year-old in tow.

I quickly found a second home at Ryan's parents' ranch, nestled in the foothills of Harrison Bay State Park—a beautiful slice of heaven on earth. It was here we established Case's final resting place. We chose a spot near the edge of the driveway—a circle of red rock in front of the ranch home. The wind always seemed to swirl through the foothills, tousling the long grass as it swept through the hills. The peace of nature, coupled with the fresh air, always cleared my mind. It seemed the perfect place to lay Case to rest.

My parents and sisters drove to the ranch for the occasion. Since Case's passing, Ryan had given up chewing tobacco, so we decided—fittingly, if oddly—to place some of Case's ashes in his last can of chew and bury them on the hill.

They don't write a manual for this sort of thing—burying your child in a tobacco can while you tightly squeeze your newly adopted child—so we improvised. I grabbed the beautiful gray marble urn containing Case's ashes, removed the lid, and pulled out the bag holding his remains.

Ashes to ashes, dust to dust, I told myself.

I held the bag in my hands and carefully examined the contents.

How did my boy become such a small amount of ash?

I pressed my fingers together, rubbing the ashes between them, still inside the bag.

It feels like extra-gritty sand. Ugh—this is weird.

Some ashes were fine, ashy powder, exactly as you'd imagine. But other pieces were like pumice or volcanic stone, full of tiny, porous holes. At one point, I swear I saw a tooth. But, I digress.

"Can I have a spoon?" I asked Kathy, Ryan's mom. She handed me one, and I carefully opened the bag. Holding the spoon in one hand and the chew can in the other, I tried to scoop a spoonful of ashes. The more intently I focused on not shaking, the more my hands trembled. Suddenly, Case's remains were partially in the chew can, partially on the spoon, and mostly all over the kitchen counter.

I gasped and then burst into hysterical laughter. My sister and Kathy looked at me in shock before glancing at each other. Then they both joined me in laughter. When you don't want to cry, you laugh.

Dang, buddy. I hope you know I love you. I stared at the small pile of ashes on the counter.

This is weird, but you're gone, so it's fine. Right?

The absurdity of the moment hit me.

Of course, it's fine. You're dead.

Somehow, the bluntness made it easier—like even in death, we could share one more moment together—a moment that made us smile. Moments like that kept me going, they kept me feeling close to my son—a bond between the living and the dead.

I quickly grabbed a paper towel, brushed the ashes into it, and tossed it in the garbage without thinking twice.

While we were laughing over the kitchen conundrum, Ryan, my dad, and Ryan's dad Rich were digging a hole in the foothill at the edge of the driveway. It was far enough up the hill that it didn't feel like it was part of the driveway, yet close enough that we could step outside anytime and take a short walk to spend time with Case.

There was a fence close to the gravesite. Beyond the fence, a forest of evergreen trees. The needles of the trees shimmered in the sun, and the scent of pine was overwhelming. The trees eventually led to Harrison Bay State Park. It was a breathtaking sight—the kind of beauty that made you pause and think about the wild, untamed grace of nature.

When we were ready for the officially unofficial burial ceremony, Adella helped Tanner carry a yellow five-gallon bucket of dirt to the gravesite. I held Azariah and hummed softly into his ear—my singing soothed him as it had soothed Case. My sisters snapped pictures as Adella and Tanner carried the bucket—photographs I'm eternally grateful for, as Adella, now eighteen years old, doesn't remember her brother or these moments. Every year on the anniversary of his death, I ask her if she remembers him. This year, on the sixteenth-year anniversary of his passing, she preemptively said, "Mom, I still don't remember him, and I probably never will. You can keep asking, but the answer likely won't change."

The hole was about four feet deep. Ryan knelt beside it and gently placed the can of chew inside. The earth around it was dark and rich, a contrast to the lightness of the memories of the brown-eyed boy held within that small plastic container. It was simple, yet profoundly symbolic. A piece of Case left behind—a place for us to remember him, forever.

Tanner and Adella carefully poured dirt from the yellow five-gallon bucket over the can of chew. Tanner's hands trembled and tears filled his eyes. As the soil covered the tin, my heart skipped a beat. Though some time had passed since Case's death, something about this felt achingly final—like a dagger piercing my heart in a way no amount of time could ever heal.

Rich and my dad quietly finished packing and flattening the dirt, their movements deliberate, as if sealing in memories every time they firmly pressed on the soil. Kathy and my mom knelt beside the freshly packed soil, planting a vibrant red mum directly over Case's ashes—a splash of life and color that would bloom every season to remind us of the life he had once lived.

A few days later, we placed a homemade gravestone that read "Case 28 Feb 2008 - 8 Jan 2009." Ryan often took a ready, fire, aim approach to life, so the gravestone didn't say what I wanted—but it was free, and it was done, so it was fine. Besides, Case was gone, so none of it really mattered, anyway.

We stayed in Chattanooga for about two years—just long enough to settle into a rhythm and call it home. Then, another opportunity came knocking—one we couldn't ignore. My work offered me a position in California as Director of Operations, with a paycheck beyond anything I'd ever imagined. As a poor kid growing up, I thought if I ever earned $50,000 annually, I'd be rich. They were offering me more.

Growing up, we were truly poor. As a child, sometimes I wondered if I'd have enough money in my lunch account at school. A few times, I didn't. And, while I always had food despite the lack of funds, those moments of uncertainty had created a sense of scarcity in my mind. Yet regardless of how scarce money was, my mom and dad provided for us, and we always survived. As a result, the idea of extreme financial stability felt almost surreal. It was something I had never experienced.

While I hated the thought of leaving our new home, Ryan encouraged me to take the job. With the constant trials of life, I had almost forgotten how to dream about life and a future. I was treading water just trying to keep everyone believing we were doing okay. It felt good to think about the future and have hope. But was it reckless to pursue a new career in a location so far from home? Was it reckless to start over again?

It was the kind of opportunity that could change our lives forever. Yet, as with every other life-changing decision, doubt and worry flooded my mind. Since moving to Chattanooga, Ryan attended fewer twelve-step meetings than he did during our time in Nashville. The fewer twelve-step meetings he attended, the more strenuous life at home became. He didn't attend meetings as often because they didn't have a community like they did in Nashville.

The thought of moving even further away from the place that we called home, during a time where Ryan and I weren't doing very well, left me terrified. Would this new chapter bring the healing we desperately needed, or would it lead us to a place of darkness and despair? Regardless, we took the leap—worried, excited, and eager to find our next new normal.

Ryan gave up his job as a sixth-grade English teacher for me and my career. It felt like something he shouldn't have to do—give up something he loved. Deep down inside, I feared he would resent me, but he was excited about the paycheck I would take home.

That he'd graduated, let alone become an English teacher, was nothing short of a miracle. When I met him at twenty-eight, his reading was below a fourth-grade level. After a battery of tests and incredible support from the local community college, it was determined Ryan had dyslexia. With the right tools in place, he graduated near the top of his class and was teaching English—by the grace of God.

When we were first dating, we'd read aloud to each other before bed every night. I can still hear him reading lines from

The Tao of Pooh and *Life of Pi,* the first books we read together. Despite his challenges, Ryan never seemed embarrassed to read in front of me or ashamed to ask for help—his unwavering confidence was attractive beyond belief. I like to think that played a small part in him graduating and becoming a teacher, but the truth is, it was all his hard work and determination that paved the winding road to get him there.

As we jumped into the next phase of life, my anxiety kicked in and my mind filled with insecurity. Gosh, I was jealous of Ryan's assurance in times like this, even when it came across as harsh and aggressive. I hated my uncertainty and the never ending unnecessary dialogue in my mind.

What if I'm horrible at this job? What if everyone I work with hates me? What if we don't make any friends? What if Ryan relapses? What will we do without our family? What will we do without support? What if we can't afford to live in California?

The what ifs were deafening, a constant hum in the back of my mind. And yet, I marched on. I projected composure and self-confidence to everyone around me, masking my deep insecurity and uncertainty. My childhood had taught me one lesson above all—and not necessarily a good one—it's okay to feel insecure, but let no one see it. If you keep the mask firmly in place, everything will seem fine—even if it isn't.

Statistically speaking, the odds of success were stacked against us. Losing a child often leaves marriages fractured. Though we had survived the unthinkable, I couldn't help thinking that those who had supported us through Case's death were watching closely. It was as if there was a magnifying glass over us. Some were waiting for us to fail, others were praying for us to succeed. Of course, those expectations were something I had created in my mind, but that didn't make them feel any less real. The weight of the imagined judgement was suffocating. Add a recovering alcoholic to the mix whose only sober time prior to now had been because of incarceration, and you have a recipe for disaster.

I smiled and told everyone who asked that we were excited and that everything was going to be fine. At home, however, I was a mess. One evening while Adella and Azariah were sleeping, I changed my mind. I decided I didn't want to take the job—moving was too much.

"Ryan, I just don't think this is a good idea," I said, my voice filled with worry. "We have your family here to support us. Even though your twelve-step community isn't as strong as it was in Nashville, it's still better than starting over. I'm afraid that if we move, we'll fall apart."

He stood up and paced back and forth, a hint of anger and frustration showing on his face as he scrunched his eyebrows. He came closer, pointed his finger at me, raised his voice, and said, "You're not backing out of this. There's no way you are going to do this to me. You're taking the job!"

"But I don't want to," I said firmly. "I don't think it's going to work out for us. It's not a good idea."

His arms shot up in the air as he came closer to me. "You're taking the job."

"Why? Why do you want me to take the job so badly?" Tears filled my eyes as his anger rose.

He put his face inches from mine and mocked me in a childlike voice. "Oh, you're going to cry now? Of course, you are. God. You're a freaking psychotic bitch who never wants to do anything fun or exciting."

I mustered up the courage to speak. "Ryan, I don't want to go. I have a say in this too," my voice filled with worry.

How do I calm him down? How do I get out of here?

He lunged at me, shoving me hard against the kitchen wall with his forearm pressed firmly against my neck. "You're taking the job."

I gasped for breath. "Okay," I said, my voice just above a whisper.

Without another word, he disappeared for the rest of the evening.

What the heck was that? Maybe I should have kept my mouth shut.

Does he hate me? Did I piss him off? Is he going to relapse?

I think he just needs to go to a meeting.

That didn't just happen. Did it?

The decision was made. We were moving to California. And after how the decision was made, I was even more afraid of what life would be like if we moved further from home. I couldn't bear the thought of it.

We packed up the car and a twenty-six-foot U-Haul carrying Ryan's motorcycle and the rest of our belongings and made the twenty-four-hour drive to California. There was no one waiting for us in California—no community, no friends, no church, no twelve-step program home group—just a job. Would Ryan's frequency of attending twelve-step recovery meetings, already diminished, fall to zero in California? And if it did, how would I live with a dry drunk? When Ryan actively worked a program, life was good. When he didn't, it wasn't much fun. His anger stirred.

The waves of life were coming at me faster than I knew how to handle, but I kept swimming—hoping I wouldn't be swept away by the tide.

CHAPTER 15

THE COLLAPSE

When we arrived in California, I was an exemplary employee—every boss's dream. I'd march up the stairs at 7:55 a.m., meticulously complete every task assigned (and then some), and head back down the stairs at 5:15 p.m. every day. Showing up early, getting the job done well, and leaving after hours had me thinking I was well on my way.

Then, one day, I was called into the CEO's office. Although he was my boss, it was a rare occurrence, so I had no idea what to expect. I could feel my armpits sweat as hives broke out on my chest—a frequent occurrence any time I experienced anxiety or adrenaline rushing through my body. I walked in, pulled back the black leather chair, and sat down nervously, waiting to learn why I had been called into his office.

"Ashley, you're incredible ..."

Thank God. I can rest easy now—this is going to be a good conversation.

"But," he continued, "some people think you're a bitch."

Excuse me? What the heck? Did he just say I'm a bitch?

The look on my face must have said it all, because he continued with no questioning or need for clarification.

"Every day, you walk up the stairs at 7:55, get more work done than most employees, and leave at 5:15. But you never talk to anyone on the team. You never stop to say, 'Hi, how was your weekend?' You never ask about anyone's life or kids. You just work, and then you leave. It comes across as though you are a bitch. Why?"

Holy hell. As if hearing it once wasn't enough, he said it again; "you are a bitch."

I stared at him, dumbfounded, my eyes bugging out. "Why?" I paused. "I didn't think you were paying me to get to know people. I thought you were paying me to work. If you want me to talk to people and get to know the team, I can do that. I just didn't know that's what you were paying me to do."

He explained how relationships were a huge part of being a well-respected leader and that without relationships, I could not have trust. He told me that to take my career to the next level, I'd have to develop relationships with people. Of course, these were all things that I knew, so it felt like a gut punch that I'd been so stupid, so focused on succeeding in my new role that I'd forgotten the relationship aspect. That was where I'd thrived when working in the clinic.

"I want you to start with this," he said. "Every Monday, when you get to the office, I want you to stop by your team's room, sit down for at least ten minutes, and ask them how their weekend was. I don't care if you end up staying there for thirty minutes or even more. I just want you to get to know people here and allow them to get to know you."

"So, to clarify, you're okay paying me to simply get to know people?" I inquired, my strong work ethic questioning what I was hearing.

"Not only am I okay with it, but I'm telling you to do it," he said.

If there's one thing I'm good at, it's following orders. I can do this. And did he seriously call me a bitch? Twice?

When I arrived home that evening, Ryan laughed as I recounted my conversation with the CEO, waving my arms and telling the story in a much more dramatic way than it likely had occurred. He told me I could be a bitch occasionally.

I mean, he's not wrong. What I see as being firm and direct, some people perceive as being a bitch.

As I settled into my new role as the Director of Operations, Ryan frantically applied for teaching positions—hoping to land his next role as an English teacher. After what felt like forever (but was likely a few weeks) he received an offer from a local high school to be their new tenth-grade English teacher. The school had an outdoor campus, something unheard of where we were from. Ryan was excited about the campus, the opportunity, and he couldn't wait to get started.

Two weekends before school started, Adella, Azariah, and I helped him set up his classroom. He brought all of his graffiti art and his books, and couldn't have been more excited about starting his new job. After all, he'd been skateboarding around a non-skateboarding community and playing house husband for a bit longer than his liking. Ryan, living with ADHD, was a busybody. He needed to be occupied at all times, so getting back to school couldn't have come at a better time for him and for our relationship.

His first day was amazing, and the second day was too. But at noon on his third day, I received a text that said:

"They sent me home today because they are still waiting for my background check to clear. They encountered a few snags, but I spoke to HR, and it sounds like it will be cleared up pretty soon."

By "a couple of snags," Ryan meant a seventy-five-page background check that had them tied up in knots. The pages contained everything from unpaid traffic violations in Minnesota, to resisting arrest in California, to disorderly conduct in Arizona. Page after page contained a seemingly endless legal history. I was baffled. I thought his pardon had cleared all of this. I knew his past was colorful, but I didn't realize how vivid those colors were until the background check stared me in the face.

Any time I questioned something written on one of the seventy-five pages, Ryan would erupt.

"What? Am I supposed to tell you every fucking thing about myself?" He grabbed his head with his hands. "I thought you were my wife, not my mom. Now you need to know every damn detail of my life? How am I supposed to tell you everything when I don't remember everything?"

"I'm sorry. I was just asking a question.," I whispered, as though I was a puppy with my tail between my legs.

"God, you're so controlling. Can you just leave me alone?"

And so I would. We began interacting less and less because the less we spoke, the better we got along.

How did a man like him marry someone like me—a girl who had a full-blown panic attack at eighteen after getting pulled over for tapping her brakes too often in front of a trucker who reported her for playing games, and who swore it would never happen again? To this day, I'm convinced airport security is going to find drugs on me, despite having never so much as touched one.

Hello, anxiety?

"It sounds like it will be cleared up pretty soon," turned into two weeks, which turned into two months, which finally turned into: "We're really sorry, but there's some stuff in your background we weren't expecting, so we're unable to move forward with your position because the state of California denied your teaching license."

And just like that, the tide had carried us back out to sea.

The disappointment we felt was overwhelming. After all the work Ryan had done, after all of the hurdles he had jumped over, he was still reaching dead ends. Ryan was the kind of person who needed a purpose and a passion, and teaching had always filled that void. Now, once again, he couldn't teach. Just as badly as he needed to find something new for himself, I needed him to find something for me, too. The more he was home, the more strained our relationship became. He was constantly picking fights with me, and when he did, words were his greatest weapon. He knew how to use them—well—to hurt, to cut, to break me down.

It was the simple things that would lead to arguments. Such as my telling him that buying his desired, expensive bicycle made little sense financially. Being told "no" set him off like a firework. Any time he felt frustrated, his favorite words were, "You're a crazy, controlling, psychotic bitch." He knew those words would leave me in tears and I would immediately shut down, no longer attempting to argue my case. The longer Ryan was jobless, the worse our home life became.

Eventually, Ryan got a job in sales at the company I worked for, because when life is messy, why not add some nepotism to the mix?

The stress of him not having a job for the better part of nine months, combined with the newness of my job and the both of us being away from our tribe, had already taken its toll on our marriage. We were faking it—something I had become accustomed to in life—but not always faking it well.

We went fishing almost every weekend. It seemed to be one of the few things that brought joy to Ryan's life. So, even though I was exhausted, and all I wanted to do was relax, we meticulously packed every piece of fishing gear we owned, loaded our tiny white Nissan Versa hatchback—hardly equipped to carry such a load—drove two and a half hours to one of our favorite beaches, stopped at the bait shop, spent the day fishing, and drove two and a half hours back. On Sunday, we'd often pack up and do it all over again. With a two-year-old and a six-year-old, it was anything but easy. But seeing the joy on Adella and Azariah's faces as they sat in an inner tube anchored down by a fifteen-pound dumbbell, feeling wave after wave as Ryan and I caught Pacific mackerel, made it all worth it. The Pacific mackerel made the perfect dinner, and it made each day a little brighter.

On one particular day, Ryan was in one of his moods— the kind where everyone in the room immediately knew he was off. The kind that settled over him like a dark cloud. The tension was palpable. I didn't know whether to speak up or remain silent. Every move felt calculated. When Ryan was in one of these moods, we followed his lead with a near militant obedience. Whatever he wanted to do, we did it. Wherever he wanted to be, we followed (if he wanted us there).

As if in alignment with his mood, the day unraveled in perfect disharmony. We fished for hours without a single bite. Azariah missed his nap, grew cranky, and let everyone in the family know he wasn't having it. Issues kept popping up until it was almost impossible to ignore them. The tension swelled; the tide was about to break.

After hours of the fish not biting, Ryan decided it was time to call it quits. We packed the vehicle up quickly, cranky kids in tow, and began the drive home. You could cut the tension with a knife. As we approached the dreaded I-5—the highway notorious for making any bad day worse—Ryan snapped. His voice erupted, filling the small space of the car as he shouted about how all he'd wanted was one simple thing: to fish, and *we* hadn't allowed that to happen.

I sat there, unfazed. By this point, I was so accustomed to these explosions that they no longer had the power to hurt me. Every move that took us farther from Nashville had us drifting farther from church and Ryan's twelve-step program home group—the lifeline that had anchored him through the storm of his first year of sobriety. During that initial year of recovery, he had braved 365 twelve-step meetings in 365 days—a remarkable and necessary feat to stay sober through challenging times. Now, his meeting attendance was so infrequent—maybe once every few months—that I hardly noticed when he was gone. The distance between us, both physical and emotional, was widening. And as the gap extended, the fear within me grew.

As Ryan's rant continued, I turned to him and said, "Then pull over and fish. I'll watch the kids in the car." It wasn't what I wanted to do, but it's what I needed to do to escape the moment.

Ryan didn't hesitate. At the first sign of water on the edge of the road, he pulled over, found a parking spot, frantically grabbed his pole, and stormed to the water. For a moment, there was peace in the car as the kids slept and Ryan fished, but as I sat there watching him cast and reel the line in time after time, my anger rose. Every cast filled me with more and more resentment. I would do anything to keep him happy, anything to keep him sober, but at what cost?

Ryan fished until the sun set, and we returned home empty-handed. The drive was agonizing. It was usually a manageable two hours, but as traffic slowed to a crawl, it stretched to a tortuous four. Every minute felt like a reminder of the day's disappointments—no fish, no fun, no laughter, no smiles. Something inside of me changed that day. It's a day I'll remember forever, but one I desperately wish I could forget.

From that day forward, our relationship was different. I carefully selected my words any time we talked, and I rarely voiced my desires and needs. It was almost like I was holding my breath, waiting for the next explosion to happen or the next fight to commence. Eventually, it became easier to avoid each other altogether. You can't argue with someone you don't see or talk to. On the weekends, instead of heading off to go fishing with Ryan, I started taking the kids to the community pool. I figured maybe some time alone would help Ryan find peace. The world felt increasingly out of my control. Deep down, I knew our relationship hadn't just run ashore. We had capsized, caught in divergent tides, drifting further and further apart with every day.

I don't remember exactly what sparked the argument that would become the beginning of the end, but I recall the topics—finances, bills, and how we were spending money. I felt like we were living above our means, but Ryan was enjoying the splendor of my increased paycheck. The more I worried about the future, the more he seemed to indulge in the present. I felt like we were on two different paths, and I had no idea how to get us back on the same one.

One day, in the heat of an argument, I snapped. I looked at him and abruptly said, "We need to get divorced."

His response hit me like a slap in the face, jerking me back into reality. "Go ahead and divorce me, but when you do, I will flee and go to Germany, and our children will be raised without a father. For the rest of their life, they'll wonder who their father was."

Ryan had a way with words. A way of making you believe he had the power to move heaven and earth. In the beginning, it drew me toward him. At the end, it enabled our demise. He could convince anyone of anything, and in that moment, I knew he wasn't just speaking out of anger. I knew he would follow through. The thought of my children growing up without him hit me like a gut punch. But I wasn't about to back down.

I looked him in the eye and calmly said, "That's fine. We can stay married, but from this moment on, this relationship is over."

One night, Ryan came home with Wild Blue Premium Blueberry Lager. My stomach dropped. I felt horrified because I thought it meant he had relapsed.

"Don't look at me like that," he said, shaking his head. "It's not for me, it's for you. You're so uptight all the time, you need something to take the edge off."

"Take the edge off of what? Our constant arguments?" Sarcasm filled my voice as I rolled my eyes, yet hardly looked up from the bills I was paying.

His expression darkened. "See, this is exactly what I mean. You twist everything. No wonder I can't stand being around you anymore. You're a miserable, bitter control freak."

I exhaled sharply. "I told you I wasn't doing this anymore, and I meant it. I am not going to fight. Maybe it's time we follow through and file for divorce."

His jaw clenched. In one swift motion, he stood up, towering over me as I sat at the kitchen table. My breath caught in my throat as his eyes nearly pierced my skin.

"If you even think about filing for divorce, I swear to God, I will make your life—and the kids' lives—a living hell." His voice was firm, angry and sent chills down my spine. "You think you can just walk away? No. I will destroy you. I will take everything you have. You won't have help with the kids, and you sure as hell won't have your sanity. Try me. See what happens."

It was then that I started drinking a beer before bed at night—something to forget about life for a while. The Wild Blue Premium Blueberry Lager helped me sleep like a baby. Probably because it was 8 percent alcohol by volume. I hadn't slept this well since I stopped taking Benadryl to sleep between Case's treatments.

Eventually, I reached a point where it seemed like there was only one option left: moving back to Chattanooga where we'd be close to his family again. It was a last ditch effort, as though somehow being close to something familiar might help put back together the puzzle that had fallen apart in front of our eyes. I was desperate, so I requested approval for my position to be remote. I hoped it would help us find our way. My request was quickly approved, and I felt a glimmer of hope. Finally, we'd have a chance to reset, a chance to get back to normal.

What's normal, again?

Deep down, I knew the distance between Ryan and me was far too wide. The damage had already been done. There were too many words that cut too deep, too many angry glances, and too many moments of silence when we should have been connecting.

We let our grief push us apart instead of bringing us together. It felt desolate. It weighed on me in ways I cannot articulate. We were just two people, stumbling through life, unsure of how we'd gotten to where we were. We had no idea where we were going or where we wanted to be. We were lost. Yet, somehow in the midst of it all, Adella and Azariah were thriving, so not all hope was lost.

PART 3

THE SCANDAL

2013 – 2020

CHAPTER 16

THE AFFAIR

The transition to remote work went smoothly. The friendships I had made at work continued, and thanks to Zoom, I could maintain daily face-to-face contact with my team.

The transition with Ryan, however, didn't go quite as well. Whether I meant what I said when I told him, "That's fine. We can stay married, but from this moment on, this relationship is over," didn't really matter. We were drifting further apart with each passing day.

My withdrawal from the relationship gave Ryan a sense of independence. While he appreciated being able to do whatever he wanted whenever he wanted, I don't think he fully grasped the level of my emotional detachment. We were cordial toward each other, but there was no love, or even a genuine, caring relationship. We were just two people co-parenting and sharing space.

Ryan and his best friend, Billy, would go hunting regularly. As he walked out the door, he would shout, "Bye, I'm going hunting," and not even bother to wait for a response.

Great. I won't have to deal with you being mad or angry then.

He spent more and more time hunting, disappearing into the tree-covered hills for hours, while I poured myself deeper into work—hosting inspirational events, building connections with coworkers, and climbing the professional ladder with relentless determination. We both had our drug of choice: his to opioids he no longer used, mine to work I couldn't put down. The more I dedicated myself to my job, the more I fell in love with it. I felt like there was no challenge I couldn't overcome. Need an operations manual? I'd write it. Want a new learning management system? I'd design it. Need someone to lead training and development for a team? That was me. Need a multi-million-dollar budget? I've got it. The harder I worked, the more accolades I received, and as someone whose love language was words of affirmation, I thrived on the praise. Each compliment was like a high, fueling my sense of self-worth and distracting me from my non-existent relationship at home.

One day, while taking a break from work, I went through my flip phone to clear out contacts I no longer needed. Memories flooded my mind as seeing the names in my phone brought a smile to my face. Some memories were vivid, others were faint, and on occasion, there was a name I didn't recognize.

Who on earth is this? I wondered as I scrolled past unfamiliar names.

Then I paused as I read Dominic Phillip Blackmore.

A smile spread across my face as my mind danced back to 2005. Dominic and I dated briefly in college, and although our relationship was short-lived, the memories were not. He was tall—six-foot-four—with dark hair and striking green eyes that instantly said, "This guy is trouble." What made him trouble also made him incredibly fun. His personality was bold, edgy, mysterious, and amusing. His sense of humor was witty and dark. His smile lit up any room that he walked into—trouble with a capital T.

Gosh, he was fun! What is he up to these days? Where has life brought him? Is he married? Single? Is he happy?

I couldn't get him off of my mind. I tried to push the thoughts aside, but they returned time after time. Eventually, I couldn't resist. I picked up my phone and sent a text. "Hey Dominic, it's Ashley. It's been a while. I hope life is well. What are you up to these days? Rich and famous yet?"

To decrease my guilt, I texted my friends Jolyn and Kayla too. Seeing Dominic's name brought back all of the memories of my college days—days that Jolyn and Kayla were part of. Memories of late night laughter, copious amounts of alcohol, and the times where it felt like the world was ours for the taking.

The text conversation started out simple. We caught up on life and what had happened since 2005. I filled him in on the big events—getting married, Adella, Case, adopting Azariah, moving, and landing in Chattanooga. Over time, the texts became more frequent. Simple messages like "Hey, how's your day going?" or "I hope you have a great night." became normal. Every time I received a text from Dominic, it felt great to know he was thinking about me, but I knew it was starting to cross a line. I knew I shouldn't be interacting with a past love interest while I was still married. Yet, I continued on.

Ryan had taken off from work early to go hunting, a regular occurrence. Dominic suggested a call. I felt a lump in my throat, my chest got hot, hives breaking out around my neck as they always do when I'm nervous. "Ok." I texted back.

The phone rang. And I just stared at it.

Pick up the phone, Ashley.

"Hello."

"Hello. It's good to finally hear your voice again," he said.

Ah—there it is. The voice. The incredibly sexy voice. Hearing him immediately took me back to 2005.

"Are you there?" he asked. Apparently, I hesitated too long.

"Yes. I'm here. It's good to hear your voice too."

Deep down, I knew the conversation was wrong. I knew it wouldn't lead anywhere good, but I had to keep going. I couldn't stop. Dominic was like a drug for me—he always had been. And hearing that voice had me craving every single piece of him again. I knew it was trouble. But I did it anyway.

We caught up on life for over an hour. Laughing until we cried. Sharing stories of our kids and parenting fails. It was like we hadn't missed a beat. Something about it just felt right.

With Ryan and I both working from home, phone calls between Dominic and me were kept to a minimum, so we relied on text messages as our primary form of communication. Soon, our text messages crossed a line too. They became more intimate and provocative. Once again, I knew they were wrong, but I couldn't stop. The rush of keeping a secret was exhilarating.

We developed a sort of code. I believe Dominic came up with it. Whenever we ended a message with a hashtag, it meant the conversation needed to end until I restarted it. It would go something like, "My day was incredible, but it would have been better if you were here. #bye." Or a sexual innuendo such as, "That's what she said. HASHTAG." He knew exactly when a hashtag, in word or symbol, appeared, it meant no response until I reached out again.

"I wish I could see you." He texted.

"Me too." I replied.

"Oh, the things I would do to you."

"What things?" I'd question in a not-so-innocent fashion.

Promptly followed by, "#gotta go."

For weeks, we would text and joke about how great it would be to see each other again. The tension grew each day. Making up stories of how our rekindling would go was entertaining. It occupied my mind, taking me away from the marriage that had fallen apart in front of my eyes. Ryan and I were merely roommates. Dominic and I were a fun fantasy—nothing more, nothing less.

Our secret "hashtag" code only worked for a while. Dominic wasn't a rule follower, and he definitely didn't like being told what to do. So, in true rebel fashion, he eventually started reaching out whenever he felt like it, ignoring the guidelines we'd set to keep our conversations secret. One day, when I was working, an opportunity came up for me to go to Nashville. My heart skipped a beat and I held my breath.

Maybe I can see Dominic.

I sent him a text to let him know about the opportunity. I held my breath, and I waited for a response. Almost immediately, he said, "Well, of course you should come. And we should meet up." Deep down inside, I knew it was a horrible idea, but at the same time, it felt exhilarating. I agreed, in part because I knew it was only a matter of time.

On September 18, 2013, he came to the Holiday Inn Express where I was staying. I had one rule: no matter what, we both had to be sober. Whatever happened, I wanted to be able to say we did it with rational minds.

I remember that day like it was yesterday—for all the right reasons and all the wrong ones. I heard a knock at the door.

Holy shit. What the heck? This is a horrible idea! I don't think I've felt this excited in my entire life.

I was wearing jeans and a white burnout tank top, with a lacy, bright orange Victoria's Secret bralette peeking through. I wasn't a provocative person, but something about this moment felt risque. I felt thrilled, nervous, anxious, slightly out of control, and excited all at the same time. It was euphoric.

When I opened the door for a split second, it felt like time had stopped. The world kept turning, but Dom and I froze in time.

God, he is handsome.

My heart was pounding in my chest, and it was almost as if I could feel my blood pulsing through my body. Dom was wearing a blue shirt and jeans. His hairline had receded a little more than I remembered, but he was still that same charming guy who had swept me off my feet at the mere age of nineteen.

"Hi," he said with a smirk on his face.

"Hi," I replied, barely able to get the words out of my mouth.

We embraced. I had been waiting for a hug like this for years. My heart was still racing, his cologne smelled intoxicating, and I couldn't think straight. I never wanted to leave his arms. He was tall, so I went up on my tippy toes as I hugged him, savoring every moment. As we pulled away, he placed his hand at the nape of my neck, pulled me in, and kissed me.

Oh. My. God.

I could taste whiskey on his breath. "Hey, I said no drinking." I joked, smiling as he pulled me back in for another kiss.

He laughed and said, "I only had one, needed some liquid courage to get over here."

The evening unfolded just as you'd expect. But for the sake of my husband and children, I'll spare you the details. We stayed up for hours, eventually falling asleep with my head on his chest.

Then, at 2:12 a.m., we jolted awake because of the blaring sound of the hotel fire alarm.

What the heck? Is this really happening right now?

I peeked my head into the hallway and saw people evacuating the hotel. We were on the sixth floor, a long walk of shame ahead of me. We joked, "Do you think Ryan is spying on us and sent someone to do this?" It was a joke, but deep down, I wondered if maybe it was true.

"I'll go to the front," I said. "You go to the back."

"Okay."

In mid-September, it was freezing—not typical September weather. I had rushed outside without shoes or socks, wearing only shorts and my white burnout tank top. I called Dom to make sure he'd made it down okay. He had. We stayed on the phone until they cleared the building. As I walked back in, I overheard the firefighters saying, "Someone on the sixth floor pulled the alarm."

Hmmm ...

After a few more hours of—well, you can imagine, we eventually fell back asleep. When morning came, I left knowing

I had just done something that I couldn't take back. I wanted it to be love—something I hadn't felt in a long time—but I knew it was probably mere infatuation. Worse yet, for Dom it was probably just a night of fun. I woke up in a quandary, unsure of what the hell I had just allowed myself to do.

Dom and I continued to talk, and we met up a couple of times over the next few months. Each encounter was as intoxicating as the last, and our behavior grew more reckless each time we met.

When I was home with Ryan, we remained cordial. While our relationship seemed "normal," it was surface level at best by this point; two separate people cohabitating the same space. But, we didn't argue, and that was a plus. And for some crazy reason, we decided that it would be a great time to buy land and build our dream home. My new job was paying off, and Ryan wanted to build the house of our dreams. When I say "we" decided, I mean Ryan decided, and I just went along with it. By that point, I was simply along for the ride—primarily because I didn't want to argue. That, and my clandestine affair was occupying most of my mental space.

I remember sitting in the parking lot of the bank on closing day with a weight on my chest. "This really isn't a good idea," I told Ryan. "We're doing well, but we're not swimming in money, and even though I know we can afford it, I don't think it's a wise decision."

"That's fine," he said, brushing it off. "I'll move forward without you."

I shot back, "You need my income to be approved. What if I don't sign the papers? It's really not a good idea."

His eyes hardened. "If you don't sign the papers, I will ruin the rest of your life."

And once again, I believed him. Where there's a will, there's a way, and Ryan would find it. He had this presence about him that made you not want to fight. If you engaged in a disagreement, you were sure to lose, so why try? I walked in and signed the papers.

Designing the house was a new challenge, but one I threw myself into wholeheartedly. Each day, I would excitedly share the latest draft with Ryan, get his input, and go back to the drawing board to make subtle changes. I ended up designing our dream home, perched atop a hill with a view of Harrison Bay State Park.

Ryan and I spent hours walking the land, trying to find the perfect spot for the house. It was designed with windows covering the back so that we could always glance out at the beautiful view. I was adamant that the view had to be perfect. I wanted to see a slice of heaven every morning as I stood in the kitchen to make my coffee. But despite the beauty that surrounded the place we would build our dream home, the foundation of our relationship continued to crumble. My decisions were reckless; I knew it, and yet, I couldn't stop. But I was convinced that if my relationship was built on shaky ground, at least I would enjoy the view.

I'm not sure how I managed all of this while my relationship with Ryan was clearly falling apart, but when I detach and compartmentalize, I find ways to carry on. I just kept going, pretending everything was fine, while the cracks spread deeper than anyone could see.

Building a house took up most of my time during the day, creating a busyness and frenzy to keep me occupied. Nights provided a temporary distraction. We'd settle in for two or three episodes of whatever show we were binge-watching.

I knew I was living on the dangerous side, texting Dom each night while sitting right beside Ryan. On one particular evening, we were watching *Justified* when a message from Dom came through that made me laugh out loud.

"Who are you texting?" Ryan asked, his tone trailing off like he was asking more out of habit than curiosity.

"The guy I'm sleeping with," I replied, the words tumbling out of my mouth before my lips could catch them.

Freedom. Finally, my secret is out. I don't have to hide anymore.

Oh shit, did I just say that? What in the world are you thinking, Ashley?

Ryan stared at me in disbelief. Then, without missing a beat, I tossed him my phone as if I was daring him to read the messages between me and Dom. Apparently, my filter was completely gone. It was a whole new level of negligence.

What happened next still baffles me. Without hesitation, Ryan grabbed my phone and called Dom—before I had the chance to warn him. I sprang into action, chasing Ryan through the doublewide trailer we were living in while building our house. It became a mindless game of cat and mouse, where neither of us were guaranteed to escape unscathed.

Ryan was on the phone with Dom, dodging me as I chased him. At one point, I cornered him between the dining room table and the wall. But Ryan was quick. He grabbed the car keys and bolted out the door, still talking to Dom.

The next forty-five minutes felt like the longest of my life.

When Ryan returned, he handed me the phone and said, "He was a nice guy. I asked him to stop talking to you until our divorce is final. Please honor that."

What the hell? Who is this? A nice guy? The guy who's sleeping with your wife is a nice guy? Maybe he's relieved this is over, too. Maybe we were both just looking for a way out.

I asked him if I could talk to Dom to get his side of the story before going no contact. He agreed and retreated to the bedroom.

With fumbling fingers and a pounding heart, I called Dom as fast as I could and closed the French doors to the office, seeking whatever semblance of privacy a doublewide trailer could offer.

"What just happened?" I asked.

"I was calm, but I put him in his place," Dom replied.

"What do you mean?" I frantically asked. I could hardly stand not knowing every detail of their forty-five-minute conversation. My lover and my husband, talking for forty-five minutes? It seemed like a living nightmare.

"Well, when he confronted me about sleeping with his wife, I simply said, 'Look, man, your wife didn't come to me looking for someone to sleep with; she came to me looking for someone to talk to. She wanted someone who would ask how her day was and actually care to know the answer. This didn't start as a sexual thing; it started with her looking for a friend—someone who cares.'"

Huh? Was it really that simple?

Dom confirmed Ryan had asked him to stop talking to me until the divorce was finalized. I asked if he wanted me to honor that. We both agreed to try it, not knowing whether we'd succeed.

The waves of life were crashing down on me, but I refused to be swallowed by the depth and darkness. Had I just experienced a wave of grace from someone completely unexpected—my soon-to-be ex-husband? He was normally merciless, but suddenly, he showed grace. That's the thing about waves of grace: Sometimes they pass so quickly, before you know it, they are gone.

CHAPTER 17

THE DIVORCE

Word of my affair got out quickly. Ryan made sure of that. It was humiliating, to say the least. At first, I faced the music and owned it, but eventually, like a turtle retreating into its shell, I withdrew completely. I had no idea when I'd be ready to reenter the real world—or if I ever would be.

We tried to make it work, or at least went through the motions. We attended intensive marriage counseling and even went to a marriage retreat in Salt Lake City. I cut off all communication with Dom cold turkey, in part because of Ryan's request and in part because of the guidance of our marriage counselor. Ignoring my demons instead of facing them head-on felt like torture.

At the end of the marriage retreat, the counselor pulled me aside. "Ashley, I want to speak to you as if you were my daughter," he said. "If you were my daughter, I would tell you to run far, run fast, and never look back. If he treats you like that in front of me, I can't imagine what your life behind closed doors is like."

I'm not sharing this to put all the blame on Ryan. After all, I had withdrawn and had an affair. But at that moment, I had never felt more validated. I wasn't crazy. I wasn't making this up in my head. It was as bad as I thought. And at that moment, I was sad because I knew it was over.

Ryan was too angry and hurt, and I was too detached. Neither of us had the will to try anymore. We filed for divorce, and I found an apartment in town. We didn't argue about how we were going to split our assets. Ryan wanted the house (even though he couldn't afford it), so I willingly walked away. One financial crisis averted. All I wanted were two couches, half of the money in our bank accounts, and equal time with our kids. Getting out of a dysfunctional environment—and away from Ryan—was the real win in my mind.

We agreed to share custody, so Adella and Azariah spent half their time with me and half with Ryan, who stayed in the doublewide trailer on the hill above the gas station while he continued building the dream home I'd never set foot in.

The hardest part of the divorce was losing Ryan's family. Ryan's parents and brother had become closer to me than my family, and suddenly, it felt like they had disowned me.

Instead of making the beautiful twenty-minute drive to their ranch every Tuesday night to watch *The Voice,* I sat alone in my apartment. I missed family dinners, the smell of homemade popcorn, and the heated debates about who was the best singer that evening. But more than anything else, I missed the camaraderie and friendship. I hadn't realized how much they'd become my friends, even more than my family. Now, because of my actions, they were neither. This was a repercussion I hadn't fully thought through before jumping into bed with Dom.

One day, I sat on the front porch steps of Ryan's parents' ranch, waiting to pick up the kids and staring toward Case's grave. The gravity of everything weighed heavy on my shoulders—the mistakes I'd made, the life I'd let crumble, and the people I'd hurt. Ryan's mom stepped outside. Her expression was unreadable at first, but it quickly shifted to anger. I deserved it, but that didn't soften the sting.

What hit me hardest was the fact that this was the same woman who had told me on at least three separate occasions to divorce her son. That day, I finally broke the silence. "I'm confused. You told me to divorce him three times."

"I told you to divorce him," she fired back, "not sleep with another man."

Touché, Kathy. Touché.

The second hardest part of the divorce was watching Ryan lose seven years of hard-earned sobriety that had been a gift from God for our family. It was the longest bout of sobriety he had experienced in his adult life. The only other long stint occurred during his fifteen months in prison prior to us meeting at the Outback Steakhouse while he was on work release in 2005. The guilt of his relapse consumed me—as though I was personally responsible for his picking up the bottle. As though our moves and my choices led him to drink again.

His friend Billy always kept me in the loop whether Ryan was on a sober streak or a not-so-sober streak. He seemed to jump on and off the wagon pretty quickly, always seeming to keep it together for a few days when he had the kids. At least, at first.

By that time, I was drowning in shame. I didn't want to slander Ryan, so I kept everything bottled up and retreated deeper into my turtle shell. Having gotten married at just twenty-one, I didn't know how to navigate life without a partner.

During the summer of 2014, I moved back to my hometown and began seeing Dom again. He became my sounding board, my safe person, and—more than anything—my friend. I could talk to him about anything, for any reason, without fear of judgment. For the first time in what felt like forever, I felt truly seen.

Because I was a married woman when Dom and I reconnected, I was a dirty little secret in his life. No one knew about me, and I didn't dare push him to change that even though the cat was out of the bag. And when I say dirty little secret, I mean it literally—there were moments where he had me hide in his walk-in closet so that his mom, dad, or friends wouldn't know I was there.

Once, I sat on the floor of his walk-in closet as he and his dad spoke upstairs. I could hear every detail of their conversation. His dad had shown up unexpectedly, and I had no choice but to make a mad dash to the basement so we wouldn't be "found out."

If Ryan knows, what are we hiding from?

I sat there for over an hour, eventually texting Dom to find out what was going on and if I needed to find a way out of the house altogether. He didn't respond.

This was not the excitement I felt when things began. It was suffocating, humiliating, and a very stark reminder of the position I had put myself in. Yet, somehow, I stayed—longing for connection and not quite ready to let go.

In July 2014, the divorce was finalized, and we finally felt free to show our relationship to the world. I felt a glimmer of hope for the first time in ages—maybe I could be happy in the long run. Dom made me laugh, smile, and feel alive in ways I hadn't experienced before. It was like rediscovering parts of myself I thought were lost forever.

We'd spend our weekends in Franklin, TN, busy with baseball. Dom hit cleanup and was an incredible ballplayer—powerful, precise, and confident at the plate. He was cocky, but he could be. Watching him was mesmerizing, like he was made for the game and I was made to cheer him on.

Cynthia (Dom's mom) and I would settle into our spot in the stands, sipping what had to be the world's best Bloody Mary—perfectly spiced with just the right balance of tomato and heat, and loaded with beef sticks, cheese, and pickles. It was a full-on meal. We'd cheer like hell, our voices barely holding on by the seventh-inning stretch, just enough to sing "Take Me Out to the Ballgame." It was a slice of small-town America at its finest—hot summer days, dust kicking up from the diamond, and the camaraderie that only comes from watching America's pastime with people who love it as much as you do. Dom was the star of the show.

After the games, we'd often hang out with the team, caught in an endless loop of drinking and laughing. Outside of my nightcaps, I had never been a heavy drinker—until I met Dom. Suddenly, day drinking, baseball, and night drinking had me hooked. It was wild and carefree, and I always felt like I was trying to catch up on the life I hadn't lived. I had been too busy taking care of Case, spending time with Adella and Azariah, pouring myself into work, or watching my marriage fall apart to truly enjoy life—and gosh, was it fun.

At twenty-eight, I was getting out of my system what most people did in college: wild nights, indulgent decisions, and living in the moment without thinking of tomorrow. Was it irresponsible? Absolutely. But was it fun? Oh, without a doubt. It was freeing, losing myself in those summer nights—the buzz of alcohol mixing with laughter and late-night lights from the ball field. It felt reckless and irresponsible, but for a while, it was exactly what I needed.

One night, after a tournament in Dom's hometown, we headed to the hotel with the team to hang out, play cards, drink, and have a good time. I loved being part of the party and was always up for a challenge, so when one of Dom's teammates mentioned he was a state wrestling champion, I immediately asked him to show me a few moves.

Dom had headed down to the bar to grab more drinks, and I didn't think much of it.

When Dom returned, I was mid-wrestling lesson, caught in some kind of hold that he clearly didn't appreciate. His face darkened.

"Let's go," he demanded before storming off toward the car.

Outside, the rain came down in sheets—a full-on torrential downpour. I didn't even have my shoes on, so I carried them in my hand as I rushed after him.

Dom drove like a man possessed, weaving through the rain-slicked roads recklessly.

We're going to die! What the hell is wrong with you?

I'm not even attracted to that guy. We were just having a little fun.

Your temper is out of control!

Once we got home, he bolted inside without a word, leaving me to trail behind. Still soaking wet, I gathered my shoes and wallet and hurried to the front door—only to find it locked.

Asshole. Frustration bubbled up as I stood there in the storm.

I knocked for what felt like an eternity. The house remained silent, all the lights off. My frustration deepened as I turned back to the car—only to find it locked as well.

Desperation set in as the rain continued to pound. I checked the back deck, hoping the sliding glass door might be unlocked, but no luck. To make matters worse, my phone was still in the car.

My level of inebriation quickly transformed into full-blown anger. I tried knocking on the front bedroom window, pressing my face against the glass and pleading. "Dom, I'm sorry. Let's talk. Please let me in."

No answer. Just silence. He probably couldn't even hear me above the rumble of the storm.

I crawled inside a small playhouse in the backyard to shelter from the storm. Thunder cracked overhead, followed by flashes of lightning. Teeth chattering, I tried to keep warm. The early summer air should have been warm, but I was soaked to the bone, and it felt like the dead of winter.

I lay there for what felt like hours. Anger bubbled up in me again, boiling over into action.

Enough of this. How dare he treat me like this!

Storming out of the playhouse, I headed to the basement window. It was positioned just above the washer and dryer, and if I could get it open, I could climb inside and sleep on the couch—that's all I wanted to do at this moment in time—that, and punch Dom in the face.

My fist slammed against the window; it was locked. Without thinking, I raised my barefoot and kicked through the glass. Not exactly my most brilliant idea—especially since I was standing on a bed of rocks that I could have used instead. A sharp pain shot through my foot, and warm blood trickled down.

I leaned into the window, brushing shards of glass off the washing machine to clear a path. As I climbed through, the lights suddenly flicked on. I froze. Dominic stood in the laundry room doorway, eyes blazing with fury.

"Are you kidding me?" he shouted. "I'm calling the cops."

I didn't care anymore. I was inside, and I didn't think he'd actually go through with it. Limping, I headed toward the bathroom, leaving a trail of blood across the floor. Still drunk and exhausted, I was barely holding it together. *Could it get any worse?*

Then I heard him on the phone. He was really calling the cops. That asshole. It could definitely get worse.

When the officers arrived, they told me to leave. I knew that if I got into my car, I'd get arrested for a DUI. With no phone and no one to call for help, I lay on the bed and refused to budge. The only person who might help with something this ridiculous was Ryan—after all, he'd been there and done that, but there was zero chance he'd answer at 2:00 a.m., let alone come to my rescue while I was at Dominic's. Plus, he was two and a half hours away.

Eventually, the officers arrested me for obstruction of justice.

At least it wasn't a DUI.

My thoughts were grim.

They booked me and put me in a cell, where I quickly made a few "best friends" and promised to bail them out if I was the first one released. After six miserable hours in jail, the same man who had called the cops on me bailed me out. By that time, I was sober and had completely forgotten about the friends I'd promised to bail out.

What. A. Mess.

It felt like everything I touched was crashing and burning. Whatever the opposite of the Midas touch was—that was me. Every decision, every moment, seemed to spiral out of control like a tornado, leaving mayhem in its path.

By that time, I had isolated myself from the church that had supported me through Case's passing and stopped going altogether, embarrassed about how my marriage had ended, not wanting to shed light on Ryan's part in it. Ryan's family hated me, and I could hardly talk to my family because they were so shocked by the demise of my marriage, especially given how well I'd masked everything. I had to clean up the mess alone. The waves were coming at me, and for the first time in my life, I didn't think I could handle the force at which they were crashing down.

Who have I become?

CHAPTER 18

THE CHASE

I desperately tried to clean up the mess I had made. I paid to fix Dominic's window, reimbursed him for bailing me out of jail, and thanked him for not pressing charges against me for breaking and entering. I got off with probation and no permanent record. But the damage to our relationship was done. When Dominic drew a line in the sand, there was no going back. The fracture between us was undeniable. It was the elephant in the room.

Dominic made me give back the key to his house, which felt like we were taking five hundred steps backward. We once again reverted to being secret lovers instead of having a public relationship. I was no longer allowed around his friends or his family. It was toxic, for sure, but the idea of winning him over kept me coming back.

And yet, through it all, we remained friends, hidden in his quiet and dark basement. Conversation was effortless between us. We could talk and laugh for hours, slipping into the comfort of each other's company as if nothing had ever gone wrong. In his basement, it was just me and him—no distractions, no public eye, nothing to fear.

On occasion, for a day here or there, maybe a week if I was lucky, things felt normal. It felt like he was giving me the key to his heart and letting me back in. To this day, I'm not sure if it was real, or if that's simply the story I wanted— *needed*—to believe. When we were "good," it felt like we were invincible. But those moments were fleeting. Any time family or friends were about to show up, he'd tell me to leave. It wasn't a question, but a command: "You need to leave, now." Baseball, a once-consuming part of my life, was now permanently off my schedule.

Am I just his side piece? Why is he hiding me? What else is going on?

Dominic and I spent almost four years in that on-again, off-again cycle. Sometimes, Dominic was okay with being seen with me in public; other times, he wasn't. My family knew we were together, but his family didn't. I was always two feet in while Dominic always kept one foot out.

It was almost as if the chaos of the night I was arrested gave Dominic a golden ticket to treat me however he wanted. If he wanted a date night, he got it. If he wanted to be left alone for a week, he got it. If he didn't want to respond to my text messages for a week or two, he didn't. If he wanted me to drop everything and show up at his beck and call, I would.

Despite the dysfunction, I have many happy memories from those years. Most of them involved hanging out in Dominic's basement, either watching a game he had bet the over on (after all, who bets the under?) or playing the guitar and singing. We loved singing together—our favorites included "Wagon Wheel" by Darius Rucker, "Hey There Delilah" by Plain White T's, "Drops of Jupiter" by Train, and "Tangled Up in You" by Aaron Lewis. We could harmonize for hours. In those moments, life felt lighter, and the chaos that swirled around us seemed to fade away.

During Christmas break of 2014, I was driving the kids to meet Ryan at our usual halfway point between Nashville and Chattanooga—just off exit 80 on I-24. The long trek in both directions was exhausting, and I couldn't wait to get back home and finally have some alone time with Dominic. As I sat in the driver's seat of my car, something felt different, and it wasn't just the bitter cold outside.

Ryan was a last-minute—or no-minute—planner. Typically, I would confirm the time and meeting place with him roughly a week in advance, then confirm the time and location the day before, and finally text him at the exact time he was supposed to be leaving on the day of the exchange. But on this day, Ryan announced he was taking the back roads and requested a meeting spot different from our usual. It was a location a few miles off the interstate. It struck me as odd, but I brushed it off. Ryan was spontaneous, and once he decided something, he was all in. Even though the new location was a few minutes out of the way for me, it wasn't a battle worth fighting.

I arrived and waited a solid twenty minutes for Ryan. This wasn't unusual, so I passed the time playing our favorite made-up car game, BLOC—banana, lime, orange, cherry. Yellow cars were bananas worth ten points; green cars were limes worth five points; oranges were five points; and red cars were cherries, worth only one point. We'd scan the road, anxiously awaiting the next passing car until someone would scream, "Cherry!" at the top of their lungs. Inevitably, we'd spend the next three minutes debating who was the first to yell "Cherry!" and thus deserved the points. It was a fun, silly way to pass the time.

When Ryan finally arrived, I buckled the kids into his car, giving them hugs and kisses goodbye, while Ryan dashed inside to use the bathroom.

"You ready?" he snapped as I headed to my car.

"All set," I replied, and off we went—he and the kids in his car, I in mine. He seemed unkempt and slightly out of it, but that was typical of his ADHD-fueled spontaneity.

An hour later, my phone rang. It was Evelina, Ryan's fiancé.

Wait, fiancé? Ryan is getting married? I guess that's what happens when you find out your wife had an affair: you jump into bed with another woman without thinking through the consequences.

"The police have Ryan. The kids are okay. Kathy is on the way to pick them up," she said. Her English wasn't perfect, but I gathered Ryan had been pulled over for a DUI, and his parents were coming for the kids. Since I was at least an hour and a half away, it made the most sense for Kathy to pick them up.

Thank God the kids are okay.

Dammit. Why can't he keep his shit together? No wonder he wanted to take the back roads today. What am I going to do? I'm going to have to hire an attorney, enroll them in a new school—there's so much to do.

All those thoughts and endless to-do lists flooded my mind. Kathy and Rich agreed to keep the kids for their scheduled Christmas break. That bought me some time to get my ducks in a row.

Aware that my life was on the verge of a massive change, I spent every waking hour of the remaining Christmas break with Dominic. The kids came home on New Year's Day and my life as a full-time single mom began.

On January 6, 2015, I got a babysitter. It was just two days before the six-year anniversary of Case's passing, and Dominic wanted to take me to the local all-you-can-eat Hibachi buffet. It was our favorite place to eat. Being seen in public together was rare, so I held every second close to my heart. Secretly, I hoped someone would see us. If someone else knew about our relationship, maybe it would feel real again. Maybe, just maybe, it would convince him that I was his person.

We sat by the fish pond in the restaurant, piled our plates high, and took bets on who could eat more. Of course Dominic would win, but I pretended I was going to give him a run for his money. After all, who can say no to all-you-can-eat sushi? As we ate and laughed, for a moment, everything was normal. I dreamt about what life would be like if we continued making nights like this a regular occurrence.

We finished our meal—stuffed to the brim—and drove home. Rain drizzled against the windshield, blurring the streetlights into streaks as we drove towards his house. I shared some stories about Case and the time he was able to lift his hand off the ground during physical therapy. Dominic listened attentively. He asked thoughtful questions. As he did, tears filled my eyes. Without a word, he looked over at me, took his right hand off of the steering wheel, reached over, and squeezed my leg twice. There was a glimmer in his eyes.

Tears? Emotion? Not Dominic.

Then he looked at me with his piercing green eyes and said, "Ashley, I'm so sorry. You're so strong."

He took my hand in his, lifted it to his lips, kissed it gently, and kept driving.

My heart soared. It felt safe. It felt good. And I felt hope.

That hope shattered later that week, when Dominic was getting ready to have his friends over. He had been talking about the party all week.

Maybe this will be the time I'm invited back into his life.

Maybe this time he won't tell me to leave.

And then the words came. "Ashely, they are almost here. You need to get out of here, now." All hope shattered. I was still his secret lover.

The year 2015 was a fresh start for our family. The kids had just started a new school in Green Hill, and I met with an attorney to amend our custody agreement. I knew it was time to have the kids with me full time so that Ryan could finally get the help he needed. A four-day school week allowed for shared custody before his DUI, despite the over two-and-a-half-hour distance between us. But with the rift in trust, that was no longer possible.

Under the new arrangement, Ryan had supervised visitation with his best friend, parents, and brother. He also had to attend twelve-step meetings at least four times a week and see a counselor or therapist monthly. I put these precautions in place to protect my kids, while ensuring he also got the help he needed. Apparently, our state was one of the few where parents didn't face neglect or child endangerment charges along with a DUI when children are in the car. It was a frustrating time, to say the least.

Ryan entered a treatment program just minutes from my townhouse, making visits slightly more convenient. I prepared the kids by explaining addiction in simple terms: "Your dad is sick. Even if he wanted to stop drinking, his brain and body won't let him, so he's spending time with people who can help him get well." Adella repeatedly blamed alcohol, insisting that if it didn't exist, her dad would be okay.

Oh, honey—if only it were that simple.

It must be hard for an eight-year-old to grasp the disease model of addiction, a concept that even challenges most adults.

Adella, Azariah, and I rebuilt our life in my three-bedroom townhouse in Green Hill, Tennessee. Slowly, it felt like home. I loved having my kids with me, yet being a single mom was hard—really hard. It tested my patience in ways I didn't think possible.

Azariah missed having a man in the house. He was stubborn and defiant (just like me), and he would throw tantrums over the silliest things. Even simple requests, such as asking Azariah to put on his shoes before we left, would trigger hour-long inconsolable tantrums involving tears, snot, four-year-old punching fists, and eventually, him wailing, "Why do you *hate* me so much?" They were frequent, so I learned to tune them out despite the emotional distress they caused internally.

Ryan spent a month in rehab, but relapsed again soon after completing his program. Every time he relapsed, it reinforced that our divorce was the right decision—while also causing a searing pang of guilt, as if I were partly responsible for his downfall. After all, he had somehow remained sober for the duration of our marriage. The moments when Ryan relapsed forced young Adella to step up and become a parentified child, bearing responsibilities far beyond her years.

Even after our divorce, Ryan's dad told me, "You were like the glue that held our family together." His comment hit me like a ton of bricks. I was already carrying enough weight, and with one comment, he laid on more.

Each time I sent the kids to be with Ryan for an extended period, I braced myself for the inevitable call: "Hey, he's drunk. Can you come pick them up?" Being responsible for driving both ways meant I was almost five hours away. It turned these crises into major disruptions that made planning summer or holiday breaks nearly impossible.

One time, the kids told me Ryan drove with his head hanging out the window, puking as they hurtled down the highway. Another time, the kids survived on mac-n-cheese for three days because Ryan passed out or was in a drunken stupor. Despite having supervised visits, each incident forced me to file a case with Child Protective Services (CPS), only to get a letter saying the investigation was closed because the kids were safe with me. It was an impossibly broken system—the only way to get CPS involved would have been to leave my kids with him at times when I knew he wasn't capable of parenting properly. Of course, that was something I refused to do.

Another time, I received a panicked call from Evelina, Ryan's now wife. "Ashley. He is drooling and unresponsive. What do we do?"

Are you kidding me? You call 911.

Instead of saying what I was thinking, I remained calm and said, "Why are you calling me? It sounds like he overdosed. Call an ambulance." I was the person they looked to in times of crisis.

Each relapse became more frustrating than the last. I spent hours in therapy, pouring out my heartbreak and frustration—not only for myself but for my kids, who sat and watched their dad unravel in real time. I vividly remember the day my therapist told me, "Ashley, your ex-husband Ryan has a disease that he very well may lose his life to. The sooner you accept that there's nothing you can do to change it—and that he has to make the choice—the sooner you'll find freedom."

Accept that my kids may one day lose their dad to addiction. How does one come to terms with that? Why can't he just stop?

All I could do was keep praying.

Throughout it all, Dominic—whom I was seeing less and less—and my therapist were my go-to people for venting. My therapist offered sound advice, and Dominic listened, providing comfort and absorbing my frustration and grief. I could only pray that one day Ryan would find the inner strength to maintain his sobriety without me cheering him on.

Dominic and I spent a lot of time together when the kids were visiting Ryan, but when they were with me, I rarely heard from him. Because I had primary custody, our time together decreased. Somewhere along the way, I wondered if there were other women involved.

One night I was at his house; he was asleep on the couch. A late-night Facebook message that initially sparked my suspicion appeared on the computer I bought Dominic for his birthday.

Why is a girl named Rachel sending him a Facebook message after midnight? There's only one reason you'd do that—late-night coitus.

I pretended it wasn't happening, but remained on high alert. The women kept coming. The more I searched, the more I found, the crazier I went. There were texts from Taylor asking when he was coming to the bar. Messages from Katie congratulating him after a crazy baseball game. Emails from Kristin hidden in his inbox. Dominic wasn't the most tech-savvy man, and since I had purchased his MacBook Air and iPhone as gifts for him and helped him set them up, I knew exactly how to access his accounts.

The more women I found, the more I denied it was happening.

They're just friends. He wouldn't do that to me.

But all in all, there were eleven women, I suspected.

In spring 2016, things came to a head. Dominic was sleeping soundly in my bed at my townhouse when his phone received a notification at 6:00 a.m. I grabbed his phone and checked the message. Looking is a dangerous game. Once you start, it's almost impossible to stop.

The text was from someone named Samantha. It was innocent enough, but as I scrolled through the messages, the rest of the thread wasn't. One message from Dominic to Samantha read, "Your breasts are like two fawns, twins of a gazelle. Song of Solomon 7:3."

One, Dominic doesn't read the Bible. Two, that is not an innocent text.

My suspicions were right. He is sleeping with another woman. Gosh, I am an idiot.

Once a cheater, always a cheater. Right? But what does that make me? Will I be a cheater for the rest of my life too?

I would never do that to Dominic. I loved him too much.

I texted Samantha from my phone, letting her know I had been dating Dominic for quite some time and that it appeared, from their messages, that she had been dating him too.

We had a true *The Other Woman* moment. We looked strikingly alike and discovered that Dominic kept things straight by doing the same activities with us in the same weeks, just different days. If he took Samantha to sushi, he took me to sushi (of course I paid). If he went hiking with Samantha, he went hiking with me. It was remarkably clever if you think about it—if you want to lead a double life and break multiple hearts, that is the playbook for how you do it.

When Dominic found out I knew about him and Samantha, he went no contact. He cut me off completely. Just like that, my lover and friend was gone.

He was my everything. I didn't want to move on. But he left me with no choice.

CHAPTER 19

THE NEW LOVE

In July 2016, I traveled to Kansas City for work. One evening, after a night of drinking with my co-workers, I decided it was time to call it a night and stepped into the elevator to head to my room. As I entered the elevator, I saw the perfect man standing right in front of me—Jackson Wells Bridger. We worked in the same industry and were from the same professional network, but we didn't really know each other beyond that.

He was tall, bald, and handsome. We had both been drinking, and he flirted with me as I rode the elevator up to my room. The next morning, I woke up to a Facebook message sent at 2:13 a.m. that read, "I don't know if anyone has ever told you, but you're absolutely gorgeous. I would treat you really well."

Holy hell, how drunk was he? How drunk was I?

I brushed it off and went on with my day.

A few weeks later, he sent me another Facebook message. "I apologize for the last message I sent. I had been drinking, and it was quite unprofessional of me." The message opened the door for more conversation. We began chatting back and forth on Facebook Messenger for a few days. Those messages soon turned into three-hour FaceTime calls filled with stories, laughter, and deep conversations. Getting to know someone is my favorite part of any relationship, as it requires real, intimate conversations. He lived in California, and I lived in Tennessee, so FaceTime became our lifeline. I'd sit and sip wine while we'd talk for hours.

Jackson said what others had told me before: "I've never been able to talk to someone for three hours, but you make it easy." I was glad the advice from my CEO about building relationships was finally paying off—I was apparently good at it. Jackson filled the void that Dominic's disappearance had left. Once again, I had a friend and a potential love interest—something exciting to keep my mind off of the never ending duties single parenting brought.

Regular FaceTime calls eventually led to our first in-person meeting. It felt almost too good to be true. We shared similar views on health, family, and politics, and we could talk for hours without running out of things to say. Unlike most guys, he wasn't scared off because I had kids. In fact, he wanted kids of his own. Jackson and I dove in headfirst and figured things out as we went.

After a few months of nightly chats and biweekly flights for one of us to visit the other, the long-distance aspect of our relationship took a toll. Neither of us wanted to be in a long-distance relationship, but here we were. The flights were expensive, time-consuming, and we didn't get to see each other as often as we would've liked. Eventually, one of us brought up the topic of moving in together—a complicated feat that involved me moving myself and the kids twenty-nine hours across the country. We hit a point where we seemed to have two options: either move forward or break up, because long-distance was a real pain.

I had decided I wouldn't have another baby after I turned thirty-two, the age I was quickly approaching. Having children and caring for them gets harder as you get older, and since I had started young, I wanted to enjoy life once they were out of the house. I didn't want to be too old to do that.

During one of my many trips to visit Jackson in California, we spent the day drinking and lounging on the beach—anxiously, awaiting the elusive Green Flash, a rare phenomenon sometimes seen at sunset on the beach where a bright green light appears as the sun dips below the horizon. That night, on a whim, we discussed family, and decided that if we were going to have a baby before I turned thirty-two, we'd better remove my IUD immediately. My desire to fix my broken family took over, and his spontaneity entranced me. So, right then and there, Jackson found the strings and pulled it out himself—money saved on a doctor's bill. He was spontaneous; typically, I was not. We carried on with our night as if nothing had happened, but it felt exhilarating, risky, and electrifying to act so impulsively.

When we woke up the next morning, he asked if I was mad. I laughed and simply said, "No." Later that day, as planned, I got on an airplane and flew home.

Jackson and I agonized over the decision: Should I move to California in December? Should I wait until May? December or May made the most sense for Adella and Azariah to transition to a new school. Jackson wanted kids of his own, and having a baby with me might help solidify our decision in an extremely unconventional way. While I was leaning toward building a life together, the weight of such an important choice felt like it was entirely on my shoulders. I had everything to gain, but I also had everything to lose.

I was the one who would have to uproot my life and the kids. I was the one who would have to battle Ryan to ensure our custody arrangement could accommodate everyone. Following Ryan's DUI, the cards were stacked in my favor. Convincing him wouldn't be too much of a challenge. By that time, he was living in the U.S. Virgin Islands with Evelina and their new son and only saw the kids during the summer. A move to California would be able to accommodate summers with him, so I wasn't too worried about the logistics. Still, it was a lot of pressure.

Is this what I really want? Moving across the country is a huge life change.

Getting pregnant would certainly make the decision more obvious. And, after our late-night impromptu IUD removal, it seemed a bit like we were playing Russian roulette, despite the hours of conversation on what that meant.

While I wrestled with these life-changing decisions, memories of Dominic lived in my mind. It felt like a chapter of my life that was unfinished. His ghosting me left me with little to no closure. Silence is closure, people say, but that didn't feel like it to me. Memories of him flooded my mind—the laughter, the songs, the heated debates, the hiding in the closet, the moments of passion.

Where is he now? What is he doing? Does he ever think of me? Has he erased every memory of me from his life?

Those questions remained unanswered. And it drove me insane.

Then, one night, there was a knock on my door. I looked up and saw Dominic standing in the rain. Apparently, he had heard I was in a serious relationship and, as the saying goes, you always want what you can't have. When I saw him standing at my door, my heart skipped a beat. I felt sick to my stomach. I hesitated. I felt as though I was going to vomit.

Do I let him in? Will this mess up my life? Why is he here? What does he want?

The grief of losing him, the loneliness I felt after he had disappeared and cut off all communication, and my desire to finish that chapter of my life took over. I experienced a lapse in judgement, and I opened the door.

I knew it was a terrible idea, but in my vulnerable state—agonizing about changing my life completely—I needed closure. And I so desperately wanted to see him, to rekindle our friendship, to forget about all the bad stuff that had happened and just go back to how things were when they were good.

He came into my townhouse.

He apologized for everything—for cheating on me, ghosting me, and treating me like a horrible person. He cried as he poured his heart out to me about all of the mistakes he'd made during our relationship. It was all the emotional intimacy I had ever wanted from him, yet never received before. In all our years of being on and off, I had rarely seen him cry. We talked for hours about what life could have been if we had set our bullshit aside and made it work. We talked about what life could have been like if we hadn't endured the hurt, the pain, the chaos.

We slept together, and he stayed the night, leaving very early in the morning, so he was out before my kids woke up. As he got dressed to leave, I told him I was moving to California to be with the man I loved. "I can't do this again," I said firmly. My decision was made. I was ready to uproot my life and move to California with the man of my dreams. (Of course, I didn't tell Jackson about Dominic's late-night visit. How could I?)

Three days later, I took a pregnancy test. I knew if it came back positive; the baby was Jackson's because there was no way a test would show positive after only three days. I figured there was little to no chance it would be positive either way, but when I glanced at the test, the word "pregnant" screamed at me.

Pregnant? We talked about having a baby, dreamt about it even, but we didn't think it would happen this fast after a late-night IUD removal. Especially after I'd had an IUD for five plus years. Pregnant. Pregnant?

Though Dominic's visit was still fresh in my memory, there was no question about the baby's paternity. It was Jackson's. I was pregnant with the baby we had dreamed of. The one we spent hours talking about during our long conversations on the beach. The child we had laughed about and hoped for. The future was finally within reach.

But I couldn't shake the sick feeling in my gut. Telling Jackson about Dominic's visit would only lead to disaster. And since I was positive Jackson was the father, I kept it to myself. In my mind, it was the only decision that I could make, and it ate at me from that moment on.

CHAPTER 20

THE FATHER

Jackson flew to Tennessee to help me with the move. We packed into my tiny white Nissan Versa hatchback, the same vehicle that had taken me to California and Texas, while my parents followed behind in a moving truck.

As we cruised down the interstate, "Better Man" by Little Big Town came on the radio. It was a song about missing a former lover and wishing they were a better man. I cranked up the volume and sang my heart out. I loved that song.

Midway through the song, Jackson turned down the volume and hit me with a hard question. "Are you thinking about Dominic when you sing that?"

"No," I said as I glanced in his direction.

Oh. My. God. I think I am thinking about Dominic. How could I not?

I had slept with him three days before getting a positive pregnancy test, and the pit in my stomach wasn't from morning sickness. It was something far worse.

Jackson insisted that with the way I was singing, I had to be thinking of someone. I scrambled to reassure him. I told him I wasn't, that I just loved the song. I explained how it was perfectly in my range and fun to belt out—just one of those songs you can't help but sing. It was our first real argument.

The secret felt like it was suffocating me.

The kids and I only spent six short weeks in California, but with each passing day, Jackson and I grew more distant. I felt sick, dirty, disconnected, and like I couldn't fully be myself—because, of course, I was keeping something from him.

Eventually, the truth came out. Jackson asked me about Dominic, and I told him (the part of the truth that I could handle telling). I can still picture the exact spot where I was sitting on the kitchen counter, Jackson standing in front of me. I was gazing out the window, looking at the water in the canal. Jackson was gazing at me, hurt and confused.

"It happened during a time when we were going back and forth between moving in together and making this work, and questioning if it was all too hard. I was unsure about the longevity of our relationship," I explained, trying to plead my case.

"Do you love me?" he asked.

"Yes," I said. "I think so."

"Is there a chance the baby is Dominic's?"

"Absolutely not," I answered softly but firmly.

Around that time, I discovered that Jackson had been engaged just three weeks before we met in the elevator—engaged engaged. Ready to have someone move into his home engaged. I had known he was engaged before, but I hadn't realized how recent it was. I hoped this revelation would ease my guilt about my situation, but it didn't. Instead, it made one thing clear: we were each other's rebounds—a glaring red flag that things would not work. So, I did what I needed to do: I packed up and moved back home—further from Jackson, closer to Dominic, with my problems only growing bigger, while my belly grew bigger too.

Deep down inside, I hoped Dominic and I would rekindle. I couldn't get my mind off of him. I wanted my friend back.

Word got to Dominic that I was pregnant, and he frantically called me, freaking out and asking if the baby could be his. I reassured him I had taken the pregnancy test three days after we were together—there was no way it was his. "I'm 125 percent sure the baby isn't yours," I said.

I had hoped he would express a desire to be with me, but Dominic was no longer expressing regret and professing his love for me as he had the night we had slept together. Instead, he seemed annoyed and distant, like all of his declarations had been part of a carefully rehearsed script. The warmth in his voice was gone, replaced by short, clipped responses. His guard was up—completely. My pregnancy had suddenly made me a massive inconvenience in Dominic's universe.

To settle it once and for all and give everyone peace of mind, I asked Dominic if he would take a paternity test. We decided it would be unnecessary to tell Jackson. After all, why worry him if there was no need to do so? I wanted to put my mind at ease and get this guilt off of my chest. Dominic agreed.

I researched prenatal paternity tests for a couple of days, found a company, and ordered a test kit. They walked me through the process. But something about the phone call with the company when we discussed the procedure made me uneasy.

The representative asked me, "Who do you believe is the father of your baby?"

Why does that matter? DNA doesn't lie, no matter what I believe.

I refused to answer the question.

Later that day, I drove to the bank, where Dominic worked. To keep things on the down low, we met in the parking lot. I pulled in, texted him when I arrived, and he sat in the passenger seat while I explained the process to him. It felt like we were doing a drug deal (or at least what I imagined a drug deal felt like), awkwardly exchanging pleasantries as though we had never been friends, let alone lovers.

We completed the process and sent everything to the lab. Then the wait began.

One day, while I was leading a Zoom meeting to plan the next big event at work, an 800 number flashed across my Caller ID. I ignored it because we were in the middle of this meeting. The phone rang again. Then Dominic called—twice. I frantically wrapped up a little early so I could find out what was going on, and rushed to call Dominic.

"Ashley, what the hell? You told me the baby wasn't mine." he answered, his voice filled with panic, anger, and fright.

"Right, the baby isn't yours. What's going on?" I asked, my heart in my throat.

"That's not what they just told me. The paternity company just called me. They said I'm the father." His tone was both direct and fearful.

What in the world? No way. This can't be right. What is going on? This doesn't make sense.

"That can't be right," I said, my head spinning. "They must have made a mistake."

Is this a joke? Am I being punked?

"No, I just got off the phone with them. Call them. They'll tell you too. I'm coming over so we can sort this out." He hung up before I could say anything else.

I called the company, and they confirmed it: Dominic was the father. I questioned them, insisting they'd made a mistake. They told me the same thing I had told them weeks earlier. "Ma'am, I'm so sorry you got the results you weren't hoping for, but it's DNA, and DNA doesn't lie."

This doesn't make sense.

They offered a complimentary test after my baby was born to confirm.

This doesn't make sense.

My brain continued to scream.

But it's DNA, and DNA doesn't lie. Ashley, are you an idiot? Are you really going to argue science? Fine, I'll get another paternity test after the baby is born, but I'm not using that company ever again.

When Dominic arrived, he rushed in through the back door and gave me an awkward hug, almost as if he couldn't bear the thought of touching me—like I was something disgraceful and disgusting. He smelled of smoke, something he only did when under extreme stress. I couldn't blame him. This situation more than qualified as stressful.

Great. The father of my baby is a smoker. Gross.

We didn't touch beyond that hug. We just stared at each other, silently screaming "help" and "what the fuck" at the same time. None of it made sense. From that point on, our relationship shifted from one of emotion and friendship, to strictly business.

Dominic left, and I had the second hardest call of my life. I called Jackson. I told him I had taken a paternity test just to be sure, and that the results said Dominic was the father.

Jackson cried. He didn't yell, but the pain and devastation in his voice cut me to my core. "How could you do this to me? I gave you every opportunity to tell me the truth."

I sobbed. "This doesn't make any sense."

At that moment, I was completely and utterly broken. Both Dominic and Jackson pulled away from me completely. I was alone, again.

I did the only thing I knew when hit with adversity—faced it head-on. I researched the paternity company and found some questionable reviews. But I still felt like I had to come clean. I made a string of humiliating phone calls, telling the truth to everyone I thought deserved to know. Looking back, maybe I did it hoping that one of them would love me. At that point, I didn't care if it was Jackson or Dominic—I just didn't want to raise a baby alone. Single parenting was precisely what I was trying to run away from.

The first call I made was to Jackson's mom. She appreciated the honesty, even though it was tough. Every call ended the same way: "I've found some negative reviews about the company, so there's a chance this is all a scam. But we won't know until two weeks after the baby is born. All I can do is pray. That's all I have left."

In the middle of this crisis, I somehow found my faith again. I didn't know if God had a plan for me, but I hoped He did.

If not, I was screwed. *Jesus, take the wheel.* When you have nowhere else to go, it's easy to rely on God for direction.

After calling Jackson's mom, I reached out to his brother, my mom, my sister Kelsey, Dominic's mom, my best friend Mae, and a few others. It was the most emotional (and humiliating) week of my life. Mae and I had become the best of friends during my divorce. As a fellow divorcee, we bonded over the shit storm that happens when marriages dissolve. My phone call didn't surprise her, though it saddened her. She knew how much I loved Dominic and had been there every step of the way when he stopped communicating with me. She saw the hurt, pain, and agony as I refused to say goodbye to someone I loved.

"Ashley," she said, "I think my greatest fear is that maybe you'll just always be a cheater."

I can still tell you exactly where I was at that moment. Her words cut like a knife, especially because I wondered the exact same thing.

Will I always be this shitty? Will I continue getting myself into such quandaries?

I didn't want to be that person. But there I was.

The wait for my baby's birth and paternity test was agonizing. I clung to hope that this was all a nightmare and that I'd wake up in the arms of Jackson Wells or Dominic Phillip with the perfect life. But I'd learned there was no such thing.

Although Jackson wrestled with wanting to hold out hope and remain involved, he moved on quickly. He soon found a new girlfriend, Claire, who took my place—moving into the home that was originally intended for his fiancée, then later became mine and the kids'. I was heartbroken. You always want what you can't have. Me included. He was good at keeping secrets of his own. All that Claire knew about me was that we had been together, but I left him, and now I was pregnant with someone else's baby.

I gave both men updates on the pregnancy just in case, hoping they would care. Jackson stayed distant, and Dominic buried himself in baseball, texting me less and less. He had always dreamed of having a boy, probably so he could teach him to play baseball.

At my eighteen-week ultrasound, I found out Dominic's dream for a boy was about to come true. Dominic couldn't believe it, as in he literally didn't believe it, and his lack of excitement certainly didn't translate into deeper involvement. Jackson's excitement was muted, too. I felt defeated and alone.

At twenty-four weeks, I started having contractions. My midwife sent me to the hospital for a cervical ultrasound. Kelsey came with me for support—thank God for my family.

The ultrasound tech furrowed her brow. "Did you say you're having a boy?"

"Yes, that's what they told me."

"Well, you're not. It's a girl," she said bluntly.

Of course, Dominic would be right. Now he's going to hate me even more. Seems like par for the course of my life to expect the unexpected. This would happen right after I bought an expensive blue rocking chair. Also, where is your bedside manner? Could you break the news in a more gentle way?

"Are you sure?" Kelsey asked.

"Absolutely," the tech said, showing us clear evidence of three lines indicating a girl was growing inside of my womb. The good news was that I wasn't in labor.

I'd already picked out the perfect boy name: Holland James. I'd wanted a unique name with meaning. Holland honored my grandparents, who had immigrated to Canada from Holland. James was the name of one of my best friends and also Jackson's brother's middle name, so it seemed fitting.

When I texted Dominic to tell him the news of the second ultrasound, he responded, "Told you. God will never give me a boy. I will be cursed with girls for all the days of my life."

Wow, that's harsh. I had been so excited to give Dominic the boy he always wanted. A piece of me hoped it would be the thing that would draw us together and make my family complete. Now a gender-based letdown seemed to keep that from coming to fruition.

I didn't care if I had a boy or a girl. I just wanted a healthy baby—preferably one that didn't die. But the sudden change from boy to girl felt like yet another wave in the endless storm of life.

The rumors spread quickly, making their way back to me in bits and pieces. And, of course, they got more ridiculous with every retelling. The most outrageous? That I had been with so many men, there were at least five potential fathers, but I couldn't even find one of them to get tested because I didn't know his name. It had been a one-night stand. And while they weren't true, the rumors cut me like a knife.

Some people at work started treating me differently, their attitudes shifting ever so slightly. Even my boss made a pointed comment: "Well, I've heard you've made some questionable choices lately."

I forced a smile.

Haven't we all, Bob? Haven't we all?

I did my best to ignore the gossip, keeping my head up and staying quiet unless it was a family member or a close friend asking questions. But even though I didn't show it on the outside, every whisper hurt, deeply. Each one felt like an echo of the thoughts I was already battling internally.

How could you do this?

You're a horrible person.

You don't deserve either of these men.

The thoughts never stopped. The noise was relentless. It didn't matter that I knew the truth; the weight of the rumors, the judgment, the shame—it was too heavy to carry.

I knew from the start that I was going to have a home birth. With or without the guys, I was going to do it. After all, I was the woman who could conquer anything, and I had Case in a matter of minutes after arriving at the hospital.

I gave both of them the opportunity to attend the birth if they wanted. They both declined. Imagine if they had both said yes. I went through the entire pregnancy alone—praying and holding on to hope that somehow, things would work out. That my daughter would have a fully present father, someone who loved her mother, and we'd piece it all together in the end.

It was an incredibly lonely time, filled with shame and self-doubt. I poured myself into my job once again—the only thing, besides my kids, that gave me something to live for.

CHAPTER 21

THE HOME BIRTH

August 18, 2017, didn't seem any different from any other day. My midwife, who was normally an hour away, was in town for a postpartum checkup. She called to see if she could stop by. My prior appointment showed three centimeters dilation, so she wanted to check on me before she returned home, only to have to make the trip again.

"Sure, you can stop by," I said. *But there's no way I'm having this baby today.*

When she arrived, we went upstairs to my bedroom, which was prepped as my delivery room, yet felt nothing like a hospital delivery room. I lay down on the bed, and she checked me.

"You're seven centimeters," she exclaimed. "Looks like I'm not going anywhere—we're having a baby tonight."

What? How is this possible? I'm not even in labor.

My stomach had been tightening throughout the day, and after two previous pregnancies, I should have known that meant labor. Still, I was in denial. The longer she stayed inside, the more time I had to figure life out. But by now, I'd accepted Jackson and Dominic were both checked out.

I called my mom and Kelsey—my birth partners in the absence of the men. My kids were home because Ryan had relapsed the week prior. They were going to stay with Kelsey's husband, uncle Kyle, while I birthed a baby.

I had two names ready: Elouisa Rae or Waverly Belle. Both were unique, with strong meanings. Elouisa means "famous warrior" and "healthy." Waverly means "quaking aspen," the first trees to grow after a wildfire. To me, Waverly represented resilience and Elouisa was more stoic.

Jackson and Dominic both knew the names. Neither had an opinion.

An hour after my midwife arrived, we went upstairs.

"Once we're up here, you won't be allowed to come back down," she said.

She's crazy. I've done this twice before. I'm nowhere close to giving birth.

I trusted my midwife. Sure enough, about an hour later, the pain of contractions set in.

After an hour and forty-seven minutes of excruciating contractions, I breathed through the pain until she finally told me to push. Two pushes, and she was out—screaming before her head was even fully delivered. The midwife placed her on my chest, and I burst into tears. I hadn't cried with my other kids, but this birth was different.

I had done it—on my own.

It wasn't just about having a baby without a man; it was about survival. It was proof that I had made it through the madness, the heartbreak, the impossible conversations. I had fought to bring this little girl into a world where she would experience love beyond measure. And maybe, just maybe, one day I'd find a way to forgive myself too.

"What are you thinking for a name?" Kelsey asked softly, smiling.

"Waverly," I said. "She was trying to cry before she even came out, and she seems feisty."

"That's exactly what I was thinking." Kelsey grinned.

"Waverly Belle," I smiled.

Two days later, Kelsey and I packed up Waverly for her first trip out—the chiropractor for her first adjustment. Then we'd stop at the lab for the paternity test. I was eager to get it done. Jackson and Dominic had already completed their parts, as had I, so all that was left was collecting Waverly's DNA.

They swabbed her tiny mouth with a cotton swab, and we were off.

A few days later, Dominic stopped by. He was quiet, peaceful—different. Reserved. He held Waverly, and I snapped pictures, but something was off. He seemed guarded, and rightfully so—the results hadn't come back yet. Wearing light jeans and a white button up dress shirt with black and gray dots on it, he looked handsome. And though we were sitting in the same room, it felt like we were miles apart. His kind and gentle spirit surfaced, but his emotional guard was up completely, and after a quick visit, he left.

A few more days passed. I was sitting in the blue chair purchased when I thought I was having another boy, pumping, when my phone rang. It was the lab.

"The results are in," the caller said. "We're emailing them to you now."

I ripped the pumping cups off, milk shooting in every direction like a fountain. I grabbed my nursing pads, and clipped my nursing bra as I reached for my computer frantically.

My heart pounded as I opened the email. I skimmed the first page.

"Probability of Paternity: 0%."

I froze. Then I flipped to the second page.

"Probability of Paternity: 99.999999999998%." The name at the top of the page: Jackson Wells Bridger.

What. The. Fuck? Can I please get off this rollercoaster? If I were six feet under, things would be much easier.

Somehow, I had survived living with an addict, the death of my son, a marriage-ending affair, being arrested for breaking and entering, but I didn't know how I was going to survive this. I didn't know if I wanted to.

This time, the grief hit me like a tidal wave, taking me under. I couldn't breathe.

I made the same calls all over again. My first call was to Dominic. At that point, I didn't even know what I felt—excited, worried, scared, nervous, or a combination of them all. I took a deep breath, my heart pounding out of my chest.

"Dominic, I got the test results back. Have you seen them?" I said, my voice quivering as the words came out.

"Not yet. What did they say?" I could hear the anticipation and worry in his voice knowing the words I said next would change his life forever.

I paused, unsure of what to say. "Well—I guess I'll just come out and say it. Waverly isn't yours." I laughed nervously. "I'm not sure if I should say I'm sorry or congratulations."

He sighed deeply. "Are you sure?"

"Yes. I am sure. I read it about twelve times before picking up the phone to call you. And the report looks a lot more legit than the report provided by the first company. Plus, I already called the company to see if there could be a mistake. They ran two tests, the results are conclusive. You're not the father. I'm still in shock. This has been a total cluster fuck. I'm so sorry." I rambled on trying to process it myself.

"Okay. Hmm. Well, I guess I'm not surprised. You had a hunch the company was a scam, and your hunches are typically right. Where's Maury Povich when we need him?" He laughed in his typical dark humor fashion. "You probably won't hear from me for a while. I need to distance myself from all of this drama. I wish you and Jackson the best, Ashley. I really do."

"I'm so sorry I put both of you through all of this." Tears filled my eyes and a lump filled my throat. Even if I wanted to say more, I couldn't get the words out.

He seemed both relieved and disappointed. I couldn't imagine being in his shoes—pouring out your heart to a woman, finding out she's pregnant, then finding out it's yours—only for it not to be. I hung up the phone, doubting I'd ever hear from Dominic again. His text messages became infrequent, then stopped altogether. He disappeared once again, likely glad to escape my seemingly constant turmoil.

Next, I called Jackson. He asked if he could call me back because he was "in the middle of a meditation session with Claire."

Claire? The girl who moved in weeks after I left? Screw Claire. You have a baby.

When we finally talked, he didn't know how to respond.

"Are you sure?" he asked. Understandable, considering the chaos of the last few months.

"Yes, I'm sure. She's yours." Then I blurted out, "I knew there was something off about that company." *Not the time, Ashley. Not the time.*

I fully expected him to break up with Claire, jump on a plane, meet his daughter, and fall desperately back in love with me. But that's not what happened.

He visited when Waverly was four weeks old. I imagine it must have been awkward—a new girlfriend who knew your ex-girlfriend was pregnant with someone else's baby—until she wasn't. It had to be its own kind of agony for him, but at the time, I couldn't think about that. All I could focus on was winning him back. Why? I wasn't sure. It just seemed like the next step to make things "right."

After his visit, I felt hollow. Why didn't doing the "right thing" work out for me? The stress was wearing me down. Post-birth, I was forty-seven pounds lighter than when I got pregnant—not just from the pregnancy, but from the stress of it all. I didn't have 47 pounds to lose.

Then work dropped another bomb. They asked me to move back to California.

Now? I just had a baby. I'm a single mom of three. I need my family.

But I felt like I had no choice. So, I prepared to return to California once more. Maybe the third time would be the charm.

Jackson visited Tennessee one last time before I moved. While he was there, I got completely intoxicated. I mean, who doesn't think that's a great way to win a man back? (Sorry, dark humor.) I downed an entire bottle of Fireball, cried, and tried to convince him to choose me. It didn't work. He walked out, and I was left feeling empty, alone, and hopeless.

I grabbed the bottle of Ativan next to my bed and swallowed the nine remaining pills.

At some point, I must have texted Jackson, because when I woke up, he was sitting in the blue chair, watching me breathe. His sister, a pharmacist, had advised him to take me to the ER, but he felt sitting by my bed and watching over me was a more appropriate route.

When I came to my senses, my parents, Jackson, and my sister were in my living room for an intervention. I don't remember much—it's funny how trauma blurs those moments—but I remember anger, tears, and swearing I'd get my shit together.

Truthfully, I'd never felt so unwanted, so undesired, so completely lost. It felt like cinder blocks were tied to my ankles, and I'd been thrown into the ocean. My life was a mess, and I didn't know how to hold it all together.

Months later, we were able to find some dark humor in that moment. Jackson would often ask, "On a scale of one to take all the Ativan, how are you doing?" And we'd laugh every time.

My need to survive and provide for my kids pushed me into action. Three short weeks after my Ativan overdose, I was packing up and moving to California again—knowing all too well it was likely a horrible idea. But I had to go, and I thought maybe I could win Jackson Wells Bridger back while I was there. But, as expected, it was a dumpster fire. Eighteen months later in May 2019, I moved back home, found a less stressful job, and started over—again.

CHAPTER 22

THE ALCOHOLIC

By summer 2019, I had been through the ringer. My son was dead. My marriage ended. My new love interest ghosted me. My life turned upside down as a result of a paternity scandal. And, to top it all off, I no longer had a career that I loved. I was a mess.

The weight of everything made me feel like I was standing in a boxing match, taking punch after punch, somehow avoiding being knocked out altogether. But I was definitely dazed and confused. The emotional toll shattered me. I didn't know how to keep it together, how to recover, or even if I wanted to.

I couldn't sleep at night without a drink. Thoughts rushed through my mind—thousands at a time. It was completely overwhelming. One drink turned into a bottle of wine, and eventually, a bottle became a box. Although I wouldn't admit it at the time, I had become my ex-husband—a full-blown alcoholic. I had become everything I'd hated about him. But the thing about substance use disorder and addiction is that it's sneaky. It doesn't happen overnight. You think you can control it, until one day, you realize you can't.

I'd miraculously keep it together for three to five days at a time. Then I would binge, hate my life, hate myself, and start another sober stretch. The cycle continued. I was a functional alcoholic.

I knew it was bad when I started hiding empty bottles in my drawers so that my kids wouldn't find them. I always kept a bottle of vodka or Bacardi Limón against the right leg of my bed, tucked underneath the bed skirt, safe from being seen, just in case I needed a drink.

Who needs a drink? Addicts need a drink. Get your shit together, Ashley. That's not you.

But it was me. So much so that one time, I completely bailed on Mae and her husband, Reginald (Reggie for short) because I just couldn't get my shit together. We were supposed to take a road trip to Memphis, Tennessee, to see our favorite comedian, Anjelah Johnson. It was a night we had been looking forward to for months. Mae and I had shirts from our favorite Anjelah Johnson show, and we anxiously rewatched every single one of her Netflix specials in anticipation.

Between the three of us, there was never a shortage of laughter—the laughter that made your sides ache, left you wiping away tears, or had you nearly peeing your pants. Reggie held a special place in his heart for my kids, especially Waverly, whom he had nicknamed "savage." The two of them were always great company.

But when the day finally came, I felt too sick to even step outside, let alone make the trip. It wasn't the kind of hangover that rest, relaxation, and a few glasses of water could fix. It was the kind of hangover that took days to cure, so I told Mae and Reggie to go to the show without me and bring me up to speed after.

The truth? I was a complete and total mess. Instead of enjoying a night of comedy with my best friend and her husband,

I was drowning in the sea of my addiction. The only thing I could focus on was breathing my next breath. Yet thoughts of disappointing everyone around me filled my mind.

And still, in the midst of my disastrous, addiction-ridden life, I started dating again. By that point, even though I knew it probably wasn't the best idea to be dating, I also knew life was lonely and no fun alone, so my greatest chance at having fun was to find someone who could bring the fun my way. Not to mention, the thought of being alone for the rest of my life was my greatest fear.

That part of my life was dark, and probably the most difficult to write about because I wasn't able to be there for my kids the way they needed me, and if I'm being honest, I don't remember too much about that time, because that's how drunks are. The memories are fragmented. We alcoholics forget the horrible things we do, making it easier and easier to do them again. We have few memories, while leaving those we love with pretty horrible recollections of the things we've done.

Throughout my struggle, my sister and best friend, both nurses, wrestled with the idea of turning me in during my moments of drunken debauchery—they were mandatory reporters, after all. But Adella was always home, so they knew Azariah and Waverly were safe. I would be fine for three to five days at a time, and their worry would subside, only for the next binge to come. Looking back, I'm sure we all felt a bit confused and hopeless.

I felt as though I was completely lost at sea, stuck in a tide of grief, not knowing how to navigate the rough waters. I couldn't see land in any direction. There was no escape, no way out. Grief surrounded me, everywhere I looked.

Even during my despair, there were occasional waves of grace. One such wave came when I met Josh on the dating app Hinge. He invited me on three dates before I finally followed through. The first time I canceled, I was genuinely sick; the other times, I was too crippled by life's anxiety—or too intoxicated.

Throughout my dating history, I had learned to hate men, convinced they were mostly in it for one thing: sex. I had already gone down that road and wasn't about to do it again—but I didn't want to be alone either. So when Josh and I finally scheduled our first date, we decided that lunch was the safest bet. We landed on Wednesday, July 31, 2019. After all, what kind of guy tries to take you home after lunch? Let alone on a Wednesday? It felt like a safe choice, and safe was good for me.

I tried on multiple outfits—some too risqué for lunch, others far too boring for my taste. But likely, it was my nerves that had me moving from one outfit to the next. In the end, I settled on a black miniskirt, a royal blue long-sleeve dress shirt with a chic side tie, and classy almost four-inch heels. At five feet eight and a half inches, those heels shot me up to over six feet tall.

We went to Johnny Carino's, a charming Italian restaurant, and both ordered the endless soup and salad. The meal was superb; the conversation was even better. Throughout the conversation, we learned we were both divorced, one less hurdle to overcome. Many men in the dating world avoided divorce like a plague, turned off by it completely.

The conversation flowed effortlessly—I hit him with my usual hard questions, and he responded sincerely. Why waste time getting into the good stuff? I preferred to find out sooner rather than later if a relationship wasn't a solid match, so I always led with pretty hard questions.

"Why aren't you still married?" I asked.

He shared the story of his previous marriage in a way that sounded genuine—as if he had truly accepted his role in its end.

Test one passed.

He had two boys, and having kids of my own, that didn't phase me. It excited me.

Lunch went so well that we stopped at a spot down the road for a drink. I was in a strict no drinking phase, yet refusing to admit I actually had a problem. I figured one drink wouldn't hurt. That's what us drunks do. And before I knew it, I had two.

Josh walked me to my car, which was a gentlemanly gesture. When we reached the car, I blurted out, "How tall are you, anyway? My Hinge filter is set to five feet nine inches, and you're definitely not that tall." It seemed it was my vocal filter, not my Hinge filter, that was broken.

"Five-seven," he said with a playful smirk and a quiet laugh. "And I've been hearing short jokes my whole life, so you can't offend me." He taunted me to continue joking—something I stored away in my brain for another day. His unwavering confidence and genuine spirit attracted me—especially in his absence of height. Still today, we joke about how he had an exceptional view of my chest.

Later that day, I went to the local water park with my best friend Mae. "So, how was the lunch date?"

"Great." I replied. "He's nothing like any of the other men I've dated, and I'm taking that as a good sign. He was kind and genuine. Seems like a great guy. He's short, but he joked about his height, so there's no Napoleon complex to worry about. I actually called him out on how short he was! Can you believe that? I'm not sure how we matched when I had set my Hinge filter to only show profiles of men five nine or taller. At some point, I must have clicked 'Look outside of your Hinge dating filter.'"

She laughed. "It's best to see what kind of response you get early on rather than waste your time with someone who has short-man syndrome. Will you go out with him again?"

"I think so," I said with a smile. There was just something different about him, and it felt good.

We continued seeing each other, but I made getting into a close relationship challenging at best. I would frequently disappear at night, unbeknownst to him, in a drunken stupor, hoping to drink my life's problems away. I'd reappear a day later as if nothing was wrong. Spending my sober days with Josh and my drunken days and nights alone had to be quite confusing for him.

But he was great through every high and every low.

He would send sweet texts on a regular basis, despite my inconsistency. Knowing how much other men had hurt me in the past, he was tender with my heart. One day, he sent me the song "Whoever Broke Your Heart" by Murphy Elmore. The song implies that a man who broke a woman's heart is crazy because the woman is incredible.

I replied, "Ugh."

Josh took it as disgust, but I meant it in an "oh you're sweet" kind of way—too sweet and kind for me. With all I had done, all the mistakes I'd made, I felt undeserving of love.

Even amid the on-again-off-again struggle with alcohol, there were moments of laughter and fun. There were pockets of joy that reminded me life wasn't just about surviving. When the kids met Josh, they adored him. As a result, my internal pressure to make things work heightened. I didn't want to let my kids down—especially after all they'd been through. They deserved stability, love, and a future they could count on.

One afternoon, as my kids, Josh, and I lounged around my living room, Azariah's curiosity got the best of him. He leaned forward and pointed at a faint scar at the edge of Josh's hairline just above his left eye.

"Where'd you get that scar?" he asked. He squinted as if examining the eye closer would reveal the answer.

A smile spread across Josh's face. "Well, I was running around a car when I was a kid. I tripped, fell, and hit my head on the bumper. When I fell, I cut my face and injured my eye." He paused. "I actually have a glass eye." He said. He smirked and touched his eye with his finger as though putting a contact in.

I nearly choked, trying to hold back my laughter. Falling and hitting his head on a bumper? That part was true. The glass eye? Absolutely not.

"Oh my gosh, you have a glass eye?" Adella practically shouted from the other side of the couch as her head turned in fascination.

Josh nodded. "I sure do."

"Can we see it?" Azariah and Adella chimed in unison as they both moved closer to Josh.

"No," Josh replied, shielding his face from them. "I only take it out about once a month to clean it. Maybe someday you'll be here when it's time for me to clean it."

Azariah and Adella exchanged glances. Their expressions were a mixture of disbelief and intrigue. I couldn't tell if they bought into his story or not, but I certainly didn't want to be the one to ruin it for them.

Later that day, they pulled me aside. "Mom, does Josh really have a glass eye?"

I considered telling them the truth, but where was the fun in that? "Yes, but I've never seen him without it in," I said with a shrug, keeping my face as serious as I possibly could. "Maybe one day, we'll all get to see him take it out."

Their eyes widened, and I bit the inside of my cheek to keep from laughing.

It was small, insignificant even, but in that moment, we weren't a struggling family trying to figure out how to piece our lives together. We were just people, sitting in a living room, finding joy in the simplest of things.

I was perusing Facebook during fall 2019, when I came across a headline that read something like: "2.1 Million Dollar Miracle Drug Used to Treat Children with Spinal Muscular Atrophy."[5]

I stopped dead in my tracks.

Miracle drug? Treat SMA? 2.1 million dollars?

What?

I read the headline again, shook my head, and blinked my eyes quickly to ensure I was seeing things clearly. Of course they developed a treatment for my son's disease almost ten years after he died. They were only ten years too late.

I clicked the link and frantically began scrolling through the article, reading as fast as I could. It sent me down the insane rabbit hole of Googling the drug. I read article after article and heard story after story of clinical trial success. Children, diagnosed as newborns, could now walk—a miracle indeed.

I would do anything to see my boy one more time.

The original article ended by discussing the cost, asking, "How much would you pay to save your kid?"

That's a trick question, because the answer is: everything. A parent would pay every cent they ever made to save their child. If I had to sell my house and live in my car, if it meant I could have Case back, I would ask where I sign. But I can't have him back. It's too late for him. For our family. For me.

I was riddled with what-ifs. What if that cure was available then? What if there was a clinical trial we didn't know about? What if we lived in another state? What if there was something, anything, we could have done to keep Case alive?

The what-ifs haunted me. Drinking eased the pain, numbing me from having to relive those feelings all over again.

I experienced fleeting bouts of sobriety, clinging to them like a lifeline, attending online twelve-step meetings on the regular, proud I could hold it together yet desperately not wanting to admit that I was an alcoholic.

During one of my periods of sobriety, I found an incredible recovery podcast—*The Courage to Change: A Recovery Podcast*. The host's name was Ashley, so she already had one thing going for her, but it was her crazy humor and sheer love for her sober life made me want to get to know her, to become her friend. And as I listened to episode after episode, I felt like we were friends, like I had someone in my corner cheering me on, while addiction stood in the other corner, jeering at me and telling me to throw in the towel. Hitting ninety days of sobriety was an incredible high. I felt like I was unstoppable.

But there were many moments where I encountered relapse, and when that happened, Adella was forced, once again, to play the role of the parentified child. The guilt hurt, and I struggled to find a reason to live. Of course, my kids were a solid reason to live—but when you're in the throes of addiction, your view of life becomes skewed. I knew I was a disaster; I knew my kids deserved better—but admitting that aloud was excruciating. The harder I fought to stay sober, the more I craved a drink; it was as if every effort to hold myself together only magnified the desperate, contradictory longing for escape—a juxtaposition of endless agony.

I tried everything to take control of my relationship with alcohol—meetings, taper schedules, moderation, only drinking beer, only drinking after 5:00 p.m., only drinking on the weekends. But no matter what I did, I kept finding myself with a drink in my hand and eventually passed out on the couch, searching my mind for how the night before had ended.

Whether or not I was actively drinking, fights with my kids were all too common. I remember one day before Thanksgiving of 2019 when Adella was thirteen-years-old. She was convinced I was too drunk to care and decided she wanted to take Waverly to my sister's house. Kelsey and Kyle often stepped in to watch my kids when I was on a binge. I couldn't let that happen because of Kelsey's discussion about turning me in, so even though I was moderately tipsy and incredibly hungover from the night before—not fully drunk—I clutched Waverly in my arms and took her to my room.

Then, in a moment that still haunts me, Adella—who was a black belt in taekwondo—threw a solid right hook. Before I knew it, I crumpled to the ground, lifeless; she broke my nose, leaving me with a striking patchwork of black, blue, and purple bruises on my face. It was, without a doubt, an all-time low.

Of course, the story I told everyone was far from the truth. I told them she was practicing taekwondo, and in some twisted way, I convinced myself that I had simply walked into the line of her punch. Sometimes, facing the music was just too painful. And deep down, I knew I couldn't let anyone see me as I truly was—the way Ryan had been to me, a hopeless alcoholic who had nothing to offer but disappointment and despair. I couldn't bear the thought of becoming that person, so I hid behind my lies, swallowing the shame that consumed me.

When COVID hit in March 2020, I had ninety days of sobriety under my belt before I took my hardest fall. Suddenly, all three of my kids were home from school for the rest of the year. I tried to work full time while teaching eighth grade, fourth grade, and preschool—all while staying sane. It was chaos— complete and utter chaos. It was enough to drive anyone to the edge, let alone someone living in early recovery. Any semblance of normalcy I had quickly evaporated in the COVID-ridden world. My hard-earned sobriety went right out the window as the days and nights blended together in a blur. With social distancing, my addiction was easy to hide. There was no one to see me, no one to catch me, and no one to care.

The first twelve months of my relationship with Josh were intermittent. I concealed my struggles as much as one battling alcoholism can, so he didn't know it at the time, but that was because my relationship with alcohol mirrored my relationship with him—on-again-off-again. Even when we weren't officially together, he was great to me.

When COVID hit, Josh and I clung to each other like a lifeline, often being each other's sole adult interaction throughout the week. Frequently, we would all spend the weekends together at his house. It was much bigger than my three-bedroom townhouse, with one living area, and easier to fit seven humans into.

We both wanted to get married again, and we'd talk regularly about the complexities of making that work even early in the relationship—especially when you collectively have five kids. I recall one conversation about how we'd get our entire family under one roof some day. It happened on a day where I was coming down from a binge. I wasn't drunk, but I was feeling all the post drunk splendor—anxiety, shaking, a headache, and an overall foggy mind.

"Packing up the kids every weekend to come over here is exhausting. I wish there was a way to get us all under one roof. Will we ever make it work?" I began.

"I know. It's got to be frustrating, but there's no way this house is big enough for all of us," Josh chimed in.

"We could use a curtain in the large open space downstairs. We could easily make two make-shift bedrooms that way," I said in a hopeful voice.

"The time isn't right, and it just doesn't make sense right now. Plus, none of our kids are going to have curtains for walls. Someday, we'll make it happen, but today is not that day."

With tears streaming down my face and snot dripping from my nose, I cried, begged, and pleaded. I wanted to be a family, but I was in no place to press my way into someone's life so firmly. I desperately longed for a return to a normal life—

whatever that meant. But I had to fix myself before I could fix my family. And while Josh didn't fully understand the battle I was fighting inside, he would eventually get a front-row seat.

At the height of the pandemic, the weight of the world on my shoulders became unbearable. One day, in a desperate bid to escape the pain and stop letting my family down, I decided that if I "accidentally" passed out in my garage with the car running, at least all of this agony would finally be over. I hated myself for the choices I'd made. I hated the constant battle with alcohol that ruled my life. I needed to find an escape. When you're an alcoholic, drinking yourself to death often seems like the best possible outcome.

I bought two six-packs of strong beer. I downed one six-pack, then headed into the garage, started the car, and quickly consumed the second six-pack until I passed out behind the wheel. When I woke up, the engine was still running, and I was still alive.

Great. I can't even do this right. Talk about a complete and total failure.

I lay there, staring at the ceiling, wondering why I was still alive. There had to be a reason—a purpose. This suffering couldn't be meaningless. It had to count for something.

Somehow, the garage door hadn't sealed tightly enough, allowing a trickle of fresh air to slip in as the carbon monoxide-laden air slowly escaped. It was, without a doubt, the darkest moment I'd ever experienced.

I can't even kill myself.
Who fails at that?

On a scale of one to "take all the Ativan," it was "take all the Ativan."

Yet, I took the fact that I was still alive as a sign. It was a silent message that God wanted me alive; my story wasn't over yet.

A couple of days later, my sister Kelsey called. While talking to her on the phone, I broke down and told her what had happened. I didn't truly want to die. I just didn't know how to live. Life felt too heavy, and I couldn't do it anymore.

The kids were with my parents. The house was a hot mess. Dishes were piled in the sink, reeking of old food, and the kitchen counter was a disaster. I hadn't cleaned for at least seven meals, and empty blue Bud Light Platinum bottles were scattered across the kitchen counter and laid empty on my couch. That night I was overwhelmed with crippling anxiety and possibly withdrawal (though the two felt eerily similar). I felt completely out of control. Josh had come over because he hadn't heard from me all day, and the chaos was immediately apparent. Without a word, he began cleaning up before settling down on the couch beside me.

I couldn't sit still. Frantically, I'd get up, pace around the kitchen, then bolt outside to find some cool, calming air—only to return and repeat the cycle. At one point, I rushed out the back sliding glass door, vomited, and then hurried back inside to rinse my mouth in the kitchen sink before sinking into the corner of the gray sectional couch, hoping to disappear.

Well, this relationship is most certainly over. I feel like I am dying. Life can't get much worse than this.

After a couple of hours, with Josh watching TV and me trying, unsuccessfully, to keep my shaking under control, Josh looked at me and said, "Get in the car."

"Where are we going?" I mumbled, half in a trance, just trying to focus on continuing to breathe; a sure sign that my heart was still beating and I was indeed still alive.

"I'm not sure, but you're not staying here by yourself," he replied. "You can come to my house, or I'll drop you off at your sister's."

Kelsey was mad at me, so that wasn't a good idea. "Your house," I mumbled.

We arrived at his place, and I crawled into bed, fighting to shake the anxiety and finally find sleep. Through it all, he never left my side. I knew I would lose him if something didn't change. He was a great guy, and I couldn't let that happen. I started going to online twelve-step meetings again, meetings introduced to me by Ryan way back in 2006. Meetings that had the potential to save my life.

On August 13, 2020, after sitting through a rough twelve-step meeting in which I showed up drunk (need I say more?), I made a conscious decision to get my shit together. I knew that if I didn't, I would lose my kids, Josh, and probably my life. That was not the life I wanted. I knew God had a plan for me, even though I couldn't see it yet. I wanted to find that plan, live it, and experience the life I was meant to live.

During the call, I reached out to the meeting host, who was a counselor at an online treatment program. I sent him a private message that read: "Hi Nico, I'm struggling pretty bad, and I think it's time I get help. I've tried to stay sober on my own, and I can't. Since you work for an online program, what do I need to do to get enrolled?"

Someone immediately reached out to me. I took her call drunk. How else does one take a call to enter a treatment program? Throughout the call, I sobbed. My admissions counselor was great. She walked me through the entire process. It clearly wasn't her first drunk admission call; she seemed like a pro. Heather, if you're reading this, thank you.

She let me know I would start counseling the following day and that Nico would be my therapist. For a year, I would attend counseling sessions with him on a weekly basis—all from the comfort of my home, giving me the peace and privacy I needed while also teaching me how to thrive in my environment, one previously riddled with bottles of booze.

I sobered up. That night, we had a late birthday party for Azariah at Josh's house. While there, I told Josh and my family, "I made the call today. I'm starting an intensive outpatient treatment program tomorrow. They're willing to work with me financially, so I'm going to do the hard thing and enroll." Saying it aloud made it real. It also made it more likely that I would follow through. I had too much pride to fail after saying something like that out loud to everyone I loved.

My parents were thrilled. I think Josh was too. I'm pretty sure it was our only hope for survival.

Before I went to bed that night, I crept downstairs, the weight of the day pressing on me. I grabbed a beer from the fridge and pounded it, hoping it would numb the feeling in my chest. I knew the night ahead of me would probably be a sleepless, restless night. The worst part about withdrawal—the sweating. The only thing that helped was to have a fan blowing incessantly in my face. It provided peace, calm, and reminded me I was still alive as my hair blew across my face and tickled it from the gust of the fan.

The next morning, I woke up ready to go. There was no turning back. I had decided, and now I was following through. I stood up, took a deep breath, sat down at my computer, and started my program with my incredible therapist, Nico. My entire intensive outpatient program (IOP) was online, in the privacy of my home, and it was a God-send.

Sobriety: Day 1.

PART 4

THE REDEMPTION

2020 – 2025

CHAPTER 23

THE PROGRAM

Here's the thing about recovery: You can only find it if you're willing to face your demons head-on. And that's exactly what my IOP was all about. I met with Nico regularly and attended a twelve-step meeting every day for ninety days (then for another 365), white-knuckling my way through the first few months of sobriety.

To cope, I turned to exercise, some days spending three hours running or working out.

People don't lose their kids for working out too much, right? But they do lose their kids for drinking too much.

It seemed like a much better addiction to have. But beyond the exercise, I did the work. And let me tell you, it was *hard*: writing my life story and reading it to sixty strangers. Identifying my core values and cognitive distortions. Working to literally rewire my brain with a "both-and" mentality.

And perhaps the most difficult—and memorable—part was writing my eulogy as though my life had ended because of substance abuse. These were the opening words I wrote:

"Most of you who are here today know Ashley as resilient, powerful, and strong. She's the one who could overcome anything, the one who would get knocked down and stand up stronger, bigger, better than most. Many of you admire her strength and determination—you may even wish you had her courage. Many of you may wonder where it came from, or how one human who has gone through so much could be the overcomer of overcomers.

Many of you wondered that until the day Ashley died. Now, you're sitting here today with so many questions in your mind, so many thoughts, so many unspeakable things. You're sitting here looking for answers. If she was so strong, how did this happen?

I am here today to share a part of her story that, to date, has been left untold to most. Ashley was, indeed, all the things mentioned previously—resilient, powerful, strong, an overcomer. She was the woman who could do just about anything. If you had a problem, she's the one who could fix it faster than anyone you know. If you needed information, she could find it faster than anyone you know. She was a doer, a go-getter, and in many ways, fearless.

But there is a part of her story that very few people know, a side of her that is just as real as all the aforementioned things. A story she never found the courage to tell everyone, although on days she wanted to scream it from a mountaintop. A story that she didn't tell because it's a taboo topic, something you don't talk about, something many people don't understand and most people judge. But it's a story I know that, in her passing, she would want to be told."

Looking back today, it's striking that I started with all the things I desperately needed to believe about myself at that time.

In that eulogy, I spoke about how depression and addiction had stolen my life, how if I could, I'd say "sorry" and "I love you" to my kids. I also wrote about how it's okay to struggle and to ask for help. It became the story I wish I'd told when I was still alive—perhaps that's why I'm writing this book now.

I ended the eulogy with:

"So, I urge you: be strong. Be courageous. Share your untold stories because if you're breathing now, it means it's not too late."

When I finished, I read it through, and the tears came—raw and uncontrollable. I wasn't just crying because of the pain I had endured or the journey I had been on; I was crying because of the grace I had been shown along the way. I was grateful—for every sorrow, tear, high, and low—grateful for the chance to rediscover how to live and for finding my faith in the process. For the first time in years, I was remembering who I am. For the first time in years, I felt hope.

Later on in my program, we circled back to the eulogy, this time writing it as if we had lived a long life after finding recovery. This time, I could visualize my future. It was filled with hope and healing; it held good days and bad. Instead of a struggle to live, I finally had hope.

In Phase 2 of my program, we jumped into discovering cognitive distortions. The term was new to me, and I learned that cognitive distortions are thoughts that cause you to see reality inaccurately. They are core values and underlying beliefs you hold onto. The longer I was in the program, the more clear it became that my thought patterns had been around since childhood. In fact, I learned that most of our underlying beliefs are established by the time we are between the ages of six and eight-years-old.[6] I remember a session where Nico and I discussed my "all-or-nothing" thinking surrounding two thoughts: nobody could handle the chaos of my life, and no one would ever love me because of my mess.

"Ashley, do you *really* believe that?" Nico questioned.

I held back tears and thought long and hard before answering. "Yes, why wouldn't I?"

He paused, rubbing his hand on his face, clearly deep in thought. "You're a very smart woman. Let's say you are an attorney and you're defending that statement in court. What evidence do you have to present to the judge and jury proving it is true?"

I blinked, a bit surprised. I loved the thought of being an attorney, but being an attorney in this sense wasn't something I was quite ready for—especially in my raw emotional state. "I don't know. I am sure I can come up with something. Even my own kids seem to hate me at this point. I'm just—a lot; too much for people."

"I really want you to think about this and come up with something. I'll give you some time." He waited.

I stared aimlessly at the ground beneath my feet, hoping it would somehow reveal the answer. A couple of minutes passed. "I guess I can't come up with any real conclusive evidence," I said, my voice just above a whisper.

"Okay. Then let's start the conversation there. Any time you feel you're experiencing all-or-nothing thinking or jumping to conclusions, I want you to put your attorney hat on and ask yourself, 'What evidence do I actually have?' Not just what you *feel* in the moment, but solid proof. Because recognizing the pattern is the first step to breaking it."

As the weeks progressed, we continued going through my phase work, piece by piece. It was grueling, unraveling all of my cognitive distortions, facing them one by one. Reflecting on my childhood and the immense hurt of my son's death, my marriage-ending affair, the paternity scandal, and my alcohol abuse were excruciating. But one by one, I was confronting my demons and daring to heal.

In recovery circles, there's a saying we hold close: one day at a time. I can truly attest to the fact that recovery is, in many ways, about taking it one day at a time. But for me, the days got easier. It's not always the case for everyone, but it was for me. As I did the work, my brain and body healed, and I realized that instead of fighting my story, I could lean into it. It could become my greatest strength.

While I was never afraid of talking during twelve-step meetings, I began sharing more openly about my journey in meetings. In addition to sharing more in meetings, I began sharing more with Josh too. After every session with Nico, I would call Josh to fill him in on the progress I was making. I'd let him know how the session went, what we talked about, and what my action steps were. It was uncomfortable at times, but it was necessary. Recovering meant being vulnerable with Josh, even with the parts I wanted to hide.

As I was going through my IOP, I fell in love with the organization. After all, they had given me my life back. I loved it so much that after completing my program, I applied for a job. I knew they'd be taking a risk hiring someone so early in recovery, but I called it out during my video interview, they loved it, and they offered me the job. I began producing their podcast, the one that helped me through my early days of recovery, and I loved it. It became more than just work; it was a way to connect with and help others through their struggles. I shared my story openly, the whole damn thing, and conducted pre-interviews for others to share theirs too. Finally, I found something I was passionate about again.

For the first time, I felt like I was daring to heal and daring to live—simultaneously.

But it wasn't all smooth sailing. In fact, most days were far from perfect. My life as a single mom was still challenging beyond belief, and my relationship with Josh was a work in progress. We experienced some extremely challenging moments. Life didn't come with a manual, and I was still learning how to navigate it. But there was one thing I knew for sure: I knew how to do it sober. And I was damn proud of that.

While drinking left me numb, sobriety left me to feel everything—the good, the bad, and the unbearable. I didn't know how to handle all the sudden feelings.

My newfound sobriety put an entirely different strain on my relationship with Josh. Before I was sober, we drank together, partied together, and experienced anything but sober vacations. I had a hard time with it because I thought this was the version of me that he fell in love with—the carefree, fun-loving girl who could drink all night and laugh through the party. But now, that version of me was gone. And what remained was someone trying to figure out how to be sober in a world obsessed with alcohol. It was almost as if Josh was a constant reminder of the person I could no longer be.

One afternoon, we had a tough conversation, one neither of us wanted to have but both knew was necessary. Tears welled in my eyes as I tried to put words to the noise in my head.

"I can't party. That isn't me anymore. That's not my life," I said. "I can't be around alcohol or in that environment. I want you to understand—I love you, but I'm not who I used to be. To stay sober, I have to change my life completely. It's hard enough to stay sober alone, but being around people who are drinking all the time is like constantly being taunted. I know I have the willpower today, but what if I don't have it tomorrow?" The words tumbled out, as I desperately tried to help him understand.

Josh sat quietly, nodding at times, asking clarifying questions when he needed to. I could see the wheels spinning in his mind as he attempted to process what this meant for our relationship and for his life. And I felt for him. I remembered what it was like to not understand addiction. Back when I was married to Ryan, I was naive. Back before I knew what it did to a person. I had lived through it with Ryan, but I had also lived through it myself, and I so badly wanted Josh to get it. To see it the way I saw it. But some things you can't fully grasp unless you've lived them.

Josh had never really seen the worst of my addiction. I had done a pretty damn good job hiding it from him—keeping it private, confined to the walls of my townhome, disappearing for moments when the weight of withdrawal or anxiety became too much. Josh had fallen in love with me despite my demons, but now that I was confronting them head on, we had to figure out what that meant for us—for our relationship.

Multiple times throughout this journey, we took breaks from our relationship—moments when the weight of it all was just too heavy to carry together. It was hard. It *is* hard. And now I know that love alone is not enough to make it work. It takes work—relentless, uncomfortable, soul-searching work. It takes the willingness to face demons—some together, others alone—learning which battles are fought side by side and which are yours to carry on your own.

Six months into sobriety, February 2021, I commemorated the milestone with a new half-sleeve tattoo. My right arm already bore a three-quarter sleeve, a symbol of Psalm 139:16:

"Your eyes saw my unformed body; all the days ordained for me were written in your book before one of them came to be."

Designed to honor my children and the strength they had given me, my tattoo featured two sparrows holding a flowing banner in their beaks, wrapping around my arm with the names Adella, Azariah, and Cornelius written within it, exemplifying "written in your book."

Each child's birth flower was woven into the design—a representation of life—a red rose for Adella, a purple acanthus for Azariah, and a blue water lily for Case. Near Case's flower, a fox tail.

Since there wasn't a natural way to incorporate Waverly's name into my existing tattoo, I decided a new half-sleeve would be the perfect way to include her. This time, I chose two Bible verses (a summary of one and a direct quote of the other) that reminded me I could endure any storm life threw my way.

The inside of my left arm says, "Mightier than the waves of the sea is His love for you," based on Psalm 93:4. The outside is from Psalm 107:29 and reads, "He stilled the storm to a whisper. The waves of the sea were hushed."

Beneath the second verse, Waverly Belle's name was inked in elegant script. Flowing waves and flowers wove between the verses—a constant reminder that when my life gets stormy, as it inevitably will, the God I serve has the power to calm the sea.

Josh and I continued dating and enjoying life as much as possible. Juggling five kids, co-parenting with other parents, working demanding jobs, and living in two homes made it difficult for schedules to align, so vacations became our quality time. Any time Waverly visited Jackson for the summer or a holiday break, we traveled. We always made sure we had something booked before the current vacation ended. We visited Orlando, the Black Hills, Daytona, Bradenton, Sedona, Phoenix, and made sure we scheduled a trip to Mexico at least annually.

When we weren't traveling, the kids and I would pack up and head to Josh's for the weekend. We did the best we could to nurture our relationship amid busy, ever changing schedules, but it was hard.

In April of 2022, Josh and I had a heart to heart about our relationship. The back and forth every weekend was exhausting, even though we only lived fifteen minutes apart. If we couldn't get under one roof, we needed to call it quits. We realized that we weren't ready to combine our homes, so for a few weeks we broke up. I didn't know what to do. I felt lost, once again.

With my relationship with Josh dissolved, I began to think about Dominic, wondering where he was and what he was doing. I hadn't seen or heard from him in over two years, so I sent him a Facebook message, curious about his life, his happiness, and what he was up to.

"Hi, it's me. I am single, so I'm in a place where it wouldn't be inappropriate to reach out to you. How are you? How's life?" I hit send.

"Life is good. Sorry to hear you're single. I met someone a few months back. She's the one I am going to marry."

At least one of us can get a happy ending.

"Well, I am happy for you, and I wish you all the best. :)" I hit send and signed off.

I was truly happy for him. Even though our relationship had been tumultuous, I wanted the best for him. Yet, there was a sharp pang of incredible sadness in my soul—Josh and I were done. Dom was about to get married. I was thirty-seven years old, starting over—again.

At least now I know. The past is the past. Who knows what the future holds?

I continued on with life: raising three kids on my own, missing the man I loved, wondering what was next, and not knowing exactly where to go from here. And despite all my mental havoc, one thought never crossed my mind—drinking. And for that, I was proud.

A few weeks after the breakup, Josh came over to my house to drop off my things—Azariah's bike, some makeup that I'd left at his place, some pictures, and a couple of gifts. When he arrived, we embraced. I never wanted to let go. Letting go felt so wrong. Being together felt right.

After he left, we texted back and forth for a couple of weeks. We both missed each other dearly, and decided if we were going to get back together, we were going to do it the right way.

We bought all the blended family books we could get our hands on, listened to all the blended family podcasts, started going through blended family worksheets and talking through hard questions about blended family life. For the first time, we were both all in. By this point I had two years of sobriety under my belt, and we had been a part of each other's lives for two years and nine months. The timing felt right to do life together.

When the 2022 school year concluded, Azariah moved to the U.S. Virgin Islands to live with his dad. He always longed for his father's presence, and eventually, I had to accept that sometimes boys need their dad—even though it was incredibly hard for me. Ryan's history with addiction, his inconsistency in parenting, and his physical distance made that decision even more painful. I sent him to live with Ryan, though I did so begrudgingly, and my pride took quite a hit. As difficult as it is to say, parenting one less child made life, sobriety, and my relationship with Josh a little less stressful.

CHAPTER 24

THE HAPPILY EVER AFTER

In July 2022, Josh and I headed to our favorite vacation spot in Cabo San Lucas, Mexico. Getting away at least twice per year was a priority for us, and this felt like a much deserved vacation. On the second night of our trip, we headed to the beach to watch the sunset. There's just something about beach sunsets and sunrises that feels like heaven (or at least the closest thing we'll ever experience here on earth).

We took an incredible vacation nap just before heading to the beach. I woke up groggy and rushed to throw some clothes on. As I put a black t-shirt over my head, I heard the keys to the safe.

"What are you doing in the safe?" I called from the bathroom.

"Locking up my iPad," Josh said. "Hurry. The sun is about to set."

I pulled my black skinny jeans on, threw on a pair of flip-flops, and we were off. We hurried down the narrow path from our villa to the beach and found a spot in the sand. Other people were on the beach too, but it wasn't crowded, so that was nice. As always, the sunset was breathtaking. To the right, you could see the shadow of the hills with the sky painted fiery orange, yellow, pink, and soft hues of gray-blue. The few clouds in the sky were gray, and there was a slight haze filling the air from the ocean breeze.

To the left, there was a family enjoying the thrill of the ocean. The parents watched the waves roll in as the kids ran up to the waves, allowing them to get closer and closer each time, shrieking with joy as the water touched their toes. The tide was coming in so each wave crept closer and closer to their belongings sitting in the sand. Josh and I smirked and took bets as to whether or not they would grab their stuff before the ocean carried it away.

Josh turned to me at that moment and said, "I'm so grateful for you."

His voice was soft, and I was too distracted to hear what he said. Behind him, a woman was power walking. Her arms were pumping as though she was about to win a gold medal in Olympic speed-walking. She had a headband on her forehead and a giant black walkman strapped to her waist—straight from the eighties. The pump of her arms and drive of her stride forward made it clear she was on a mission, lost in her own world while securing her steps for the day.

"Look at that lady," I shrieked, barely able to get the words out before we burst into laughter. I buried my face in Josh's shoulder in an attempt to contain myself. Thank God it was getting dark.

As our laughter died down, Josh took a deep breath. He looked nervous. He grabbed my hand. "I'm extremely grateful for you," he said once more. This time I heard him.

"I'm proud of how far you've come. I love your kids like they're my own, and I want to spend the rest of my life with you and your kids. Will you *marry* me?"

My brain hardly had time to comprehend the words before I opened my mouth.

"Are you freaking kidding me? Is this a mean joke?" I blurted out.

My eyes shot to his left hand, where he held the world's tiniest ring box designed to be hidden in his pocket so that it could get through airport security without being noticed.

Is this a joke? A prank? Am I being punked? He would never do something that mean. Would he?

Josh continued with confidence. "No," he said, flipping open the box to reveal the ring inside. "I have the ring right here. Will you *marry me?*"

I looked at him and held my breath.

"Yes," I screamed as reality set in. Then, without thinking, I added, "Thank goodness you didn't do something elaborate or decide to make a scene. I would have been so mad."

I looked at Josh sitting in the sand, holding the tiny box with a beautiful ring inside, asking me the question that every girl dreams of, and I felt love and gratitude. He picked out the ring so thoughtfully. It held a round diamond in the center with a halo of tiny diamonds surrounding it. On each side, there were eight small diamonds—one for every member of our soon-to-be family, including Case.

For the first time in a long time, I felt hope for the future. Like I was finally entering my happily ever after.

That trip was the second time we went to an all-inclusive resort. I panicked, thinking they might accidentally put alcohol in my drink, so Josh became my built-in taste tester, trying all drinks before me and looking out for even the slightest hint of alcohol.

One night, we decided to enjoy a dinner at sea, cooking a four-course meal with a professional chef while listening to music and enjoying the views. I ordered my usual sparkling water with a lime—Topo Chico had become my absolute favorite. The server dropped off the drink and I asked Josh to smell it and taste it. He took a sip and said, "There's nothing in there. You're good to go."

I took a sip and nearly spit it out. It was definitely not sparkling water. It was definitely vodka. Josh felt horrible, but I laughed it off. My sobriety was strong, so I more than survived the taste of vodka on my tongue. From that moment on, I started watching the bartender prepare my drinks or requesting the bottle or can directly.

The longer you stay sober, the more creative you become in navigating situations. One of my early strategies was to always have a drink in hand. If you've got a drink in hand, the chances of someone offering you one drop significantly. When you're newly sober, it helps you avoid the awkward conversation of turning down a drink, because you already have one.

Eventually, I got to a point where carrying a drink in my hand wasn't my primary tactic. I would simply say, "No thanks. I am sober."

My co-worker, Ashley, whose podcast I produced, often joked about the usual response you receive when you tell someone you're sober. Typically they say, "Congratulations." It's a little ironic to be congratulated for hitting rock bottom and nearly losing your life—but hey, congratulations! We say it in good fun because we know people mean well, and truthfully, we're incredibly proud of how far we've come too.

When we were home from Cabo, we found the perfect little hunting lodge to host our family and friends on our wedding day. After finding a venue, I went dress shopping with Kelsey, my mom, and Josh's mom. As I tried on the first dress, which I loved, Kelsey (always brutally honest) exclaimed, "You can't get married in that. You look like you're getting married in Las Vegas!"

Who cares? Vegas is great!

And so, we moved on to the next dress. After trying about ten dresses, I landed on one that I thought was "the one." It had a plunging neckline—one that likely plunged a little too far for the comfort of my teenage boys, but I didn't care. The dress featured a fit-and-flare silhouette that hugged my body in all the right places. It was the perfect balance between bold, edgy, and beautiful. The train was simple and elegant, but not too long, which was great because comfort was imperative. The nude underlayer gave the dress a modern touch, while the last layer of ivory lace added just the right amount of beauty. My favorite part was the snap-on skirt that transformed the dress from a fit-and-flare to an A-line silhouette. It was perfect for capturing a sunset photograph—something I had dreamt of since I was a little girl.

When I sent a photo to my high school prom date (don't worry, he's gay, so no scandals here), his response was immediate and exactly the dramatic flair I expected.

"Hol-E-shit. You look ethereal!!!"

At that moment, I knew I had found the dress. The dress reflected everything I had imagined—strong, edgy, and unapologetically me.

Yet, amidst my "happily ever after," the chaos of life ensued. On February 11, 2023—just fifty-six days before our wedding—Josh and I were attending a health and wellness makeover at a local chiropractor's office. We were in the midst of completing the 75 Hard challenge—a seventy-five-day program developed by author Andy Frisella to help transform your life, physically and mentally—and the wellness makeover was intended to keep us on-track. While the seminar was in session, my best friend Mae called twice. I glanced down at my iPhone and hit decline both times. I figured I would call her as soon as we were home.

When the event ended, Josh and I walked out to the truck. It was mid-February in Nashville, colder than normal, and the cold was bitter. I sat in the car, shut the door, and let out a shriek—my signature way of warming up in a freezing vehicle, convinced that the sudden burst of adrenaline would help. Josh disagreed, but I digress.

Then my Apple watch buzzed. I glanced down at my phone to see a text from Mae:

"Reggie's dead. He was in an accident."

My head shook, as though trying to clear my vision. Surely I had read the text wrong. I quickly selected Mae's name from my favorites and called her, my heart pounding. I glanced over at Josh as the phone rang. "I just got a text from Mae saying Reggie is dead."

He stared at me, shocked. "Oh my God, what happened? I'll bring you home, and you can go wherever you need to go. I've got the kids. Go be with your friend."

When the call connected, Mae's voice was frantic, and her words scattered. She struggled to explain what had happened.

I asked if she wanted to meet where she was or at her house. I wasn't sure what to do, but I knew I couldn't let her face this alone. When death knocks on your door, it's unbearable, and I couldn't imagine enduring the aftermath of losing Case all alone—so I knew I had to show up for her.

I arrived at her house before she did and let myself in. When she arrived, I embraced her tightly, and we went over the timeline of events—both of us clinging to every detail in a desperate attempt to understand what had happened.

Then I did what I do best—I jumped right into the chaos to help her figure out the grim business of death. I called the police, the coroner, and multiple funeral homes, taking meticulous notes along the way. I knew that death had a strange way of erasing your short-term memory, while leaving you clinging to every pre-death detail. I assisted her with selecting a funeral home and planning a service that turned out to be incredibly beautiful.

Surrounded by friends and family, Mae sat in the front row while I monitored the sound booth, helping with the song lyrics. We had attended the same church—and even the same Life Group—before we became best friends. The very community that had carried Ryan and me through the darkest days of Case's life and death was now carrying Mae. It was a divine display of what it meant to be the hands and feet of Jesus—an oddly beautiful moment for all of us.

After the service, we gathered everyone from The Refuge for a group picture. For me, it felt like a full-circle moment—the first time I wasn't ashamed to see these people. There were, after all, no expectations to live up to.

For the next few days, I spent nearly all my waking moments with Mae. We both knew that, eventually, I needed to go back to my kids and soon-to-be husband.

"I'm only a phone call away," I told her, tears welling up as I remembered how painful it was to watch everyone else move on when your own life felt like it had come to a standstill.

Planning a wedding and a funeral simultaneously was something I never thought I'd have to do—but I did.

———————————

Even in moments of complete and total shock, we managed to have fun. Azariah was home visiting. We loved a good family game night, and Josh and I had decided that this would be the game night to top all game nights. The night where the truth about the infamous glass eye would finally come out—literally.

For almost four years, the kids had believed Josh had a glass eye. It started as an innocent joke, but over time, it had inadvertently taken on a life of its own. Now, we were about to share the truth and see if the kids would love us for this prank or hate us forever. Josh had purchased a fake eyeball from Amazon months prior, and tonight was the night we were going to use it. The plan was simple. During a family game of Jumbo Sequence, Josh would stage a sneeze and launch the eyeball into the middle of our game table. From there, we'd sit back and watch what happened.

We carefully arranged our seats at the table, selecting positions that would increase the drama and improve the success of the prank. I sat with Adella and Waverly on one side of the table. Josh and Azariah sat across from us. As the game progressed, I could hardly focus—my mind was anxiously awaiting the moment, and I had no idea when he planned to launch the eyeball into the air. I didn't know if this prank would be met with roaring laughter or complete betrayal.

Three-quarters of the way through the first game, it happened.

"Aaaaahhhhhh-chooooooo." Josh sneezed, throwing himself forward, cupping his eye while simultaneously launching the fake Amazon eyeball into the air.

It bounced off of Adella's leg before landing with a plop right between her and Waverly on the bench. It came to a stop right next to Adella's thigh.

"Ahhhh!!!!" She stared at the eyeball sitting next to her leg.

"Oh my gosh," Josh said, his hand still covering his eye.

He's not the dramatic type, but his acting is better than I thought it would be.

"This is so embarrassing. This has never happened before," Josh continued.

For a split second, there was silence. Then complete and utter chaos.

Adella let out a scream before bursting into uncontrollable laughter. She reached for her phone. "Oh my gosh! This is amazing! My soon-to-be stepdad's glass eye just flew out of his head when he sneezed!" She sent a Snapchat video to her friends, bragging about the incident.

Waverly bolted from the table, running straight into the living room to hide. She found a space next to our brown ottoman and froze. Every so often, we would hear a bit of nervous laughter coming from the living room.

Azariah's jaw hung open in disbelief.

"Solution!" Josh panicked. "I need some solution for my eye. It's under the sink in our bathroom."

Adella, still on Snapchat with her friends, sprinted down the hallway at full speed, making her way into our bathroom as fast as she could.

Azariah stood up with a huge smile on his face. He looked more excited than a kid in a candy store. "Bucket list item, complete."

I couldn't hold it in any longer. I burst into laughter. I laughed so hard my stomach hurt.

Eventually, Josh slowly pulled his hand away from his face, revealing his perfectly normal, intact eye.

"What?" Azariah said, staring blankly at Josh. "You guys were joking?"

"Did you believe us?" I said, wiping tears of laughter from my eyes.

"Yes," Adella yelled as she walked back down the hall, empty-handed. There was, after all, no glass eye solution to be found. "That was the most epic prank of all time! I can't wait to tell my friends about this. I can't believe you guys pulled that off."

Finally, Waverly peered out from the living room, arms crossed, still a bit skeptical and unsure of what was going on. She looked a little scared. "Wait, you were joking?" she asked in a soft, questioning voice.

Josh nodded, and we all laughed uncontrollably. This time, Waverly joined us.

Family game night? Success. Trick of a lifetime? Executed flawlessly. And the kids? They thought we were the coolest parents in the whole wide world.

Moments of joy like that were just what my heart needed. Moments of joy like that carried me through.

As the day of our wedding approached, my mind was filled with excitement and worry.

My life is chaotic. Reggie's death just affirmed this deep-seated belief.

What if it's too overwhelming for Josh? Things won't slow down just because we're getting married. Is he really ready for all of this?

Then, one day after work, while waiting for the kids to come home from school, I walked up to his desk, hugged him, and knelt beside him.

"Are you sure you're ready for this?" I asked. "My life's been hectic, and it's unlikely to slow down just because we're getting married."

Josh laughed. "Of course I'm ready," he said, then we hugged and both of us went back to work.

Okay. You have no idea what you're in for.

I was adamant that our big day include all seven of us, so we arranged an unaccompanied minor flight for Azariah, now twelve-years-old, from the U.S. Virgin Islands. He flew in a few days before the wedding. Our family was complete.

We tied the knot at 5:00 p.m. on Saturday, April 8, 2023, in the presence of our closest friends and family. The day was absolutely perfect. Josh's brother, Andy, officiated the service, and as the kids tied a cord of three strands, we worshiped to "The Blessing" by Elevation Worship which includes Numbers 6:24–26. "The Lord bless you and keep you; the Lord make his face shine on you and be gracious to you; the Lord turn his face toward you and give you peace." The bridge ties in Deuteronomy 7:9 which says that God will be faithful to a thousand generations.

It was a song that was perfect for the moment.

The reception was held in the same cozy hunting lodge. Our friends, family, and all their love filled the space. QDOBA catered a taco and nacho bar. We thought this was the perfect choice for a wedding meal because who doesn't love a plate of crunchy cheesy goodness?

One of my favorite memories from the entire wedding was catching a glimpse of my friend's son sneaking through the buffet line before it was fully set up. There he was, casually helping himself to what looked like the world's largest burrito bowl (possibly even two), with chips and queso spilling over the sides of the bowl, while the catering team worked around him, likely questioning whether or not he should be eating. No one seemed to care enough to say something. I couldn't help but laugh; it was the perfect snapshot of the day—a reminder that our wedding wasn't about having a perfect ceremony or capturing the perfect picture. It was about being with friends and family, embracing the journey, and having a damn good time.

We were surrounded by laughter, love, and the people who meant the most to us. The day was everything we had hoped for and more. It was unapologetically us—now a party of seven.

The next morning, I took Azariah to the airport so he could head back to the U.S. Virgin Islands to finish school. When we said goodbye, both of our eyes welled up with tears.

Ryan texted me late that evening to let me know he had arrived home safely.

CHAPTER 25

THE OVERDOSE

Monday, June 5, 2023, was a normal day—until it wasn't. I was on a Zoom meeting at work when my phone rang. It was Azariah. I declined.

He called again. I declined the call, assuming he just wanted more screen time or was having trouble logging into his Apple ID—nothing out of the ordinary. But soon after, text messages began popping up one after another:

Mom

Mom

This is very important

Not about technology

Dad just died

Please

Call

I went into a complete state of shock. My body began shaking and my voice quivered as I fumbled with my phone, still taking part in the Zoom meeting while the other attendees watched. Somehow, I answered a FaceTime audio call from

Azariah on my computer even as I remained on Zoom—my body trembling uncontrollably.

"Azariah, Azariah, are you okay? What's going on?" I cried out in sheer panic. "Is it true? Is he dead?"

Azariah was crying, and the call's reception kept cutting in and out. "Are you with an adult?" I asked.

"Yes, here," he replied, handing the phone to another person.

Then I heard a female voice on the line. I asked if it was true—if Ryan was dead.

"I'm so sorry," she stated. "He's dead." And then the call dropped.

At that point, I turned as white as a ghost, fell off my chair, and began clawing at the ground, desperate to feel something solid beneath me. I felt as if I were hovering above my body—completely dissociated. My frantic clawing was an attempt to ground myself and pull back into reality.

I kept shrieking, "He's dead. He's dead. Oh my God, he's dead. Azariah, Azariah, I need to get to Azariah." It must have been terrifying for Josh and the boys, who were scattered in other parts of the house. Josh burst into the room, trying to figure out what was going on. I could hardly talk, and I certainly couldn't think clearly.

"He's dead; he's dead; he's dead. Oh my God. He's dead," I repeated, still shaking.

"Who?" Josh questioned.

"Ryan. Ryan is dead. I need to get to Azariah."

Eventually, I got my bearings and started thinking straight. I quickly realized I needed to reach Adella before she heard the news from someone else. She was babysitting at my sister

Kelsey's house. All the while, my head and heart screamed, *No. This can't be true.* The first phase of grief—denial. And the denial hit hard.

Josh offered to drive me to find Adella, as I was still shaking.

As we drove, I frantically turned on the song "O Come to the Altar" by Elevation Worship—a favorite of mine, whose lyrics resonated deeply at that moment. The song conveys a message that if we're hurting and broken, God wants us to come to Him.

I rocked back and forth in the front seat, praying I'd find the right words. I could still hear my therapist's voice from ten years ago: "Ashley, Ryan has a disease that he very well may lose his life to. The sooner you accept that there's nothing you can do to change it—and that he has to make the choice—the sooner you'll find freedom."

I found freedom. But what did Ryan find? Death?

It was painful to think about the place he must have been in around the time of his death. Even though I didn't know the circumstances, I could imagine what they were considering his longstanding history with drugs. He was a teacher in the U.S. Virgin Islands, loved by his students more than you can imagine, finally pursuing his lifelong dream of teaching. He'd paint graffiti pieces for every senior graduating from his English class. The students adored him.

Where was he when he died? What was he doing? I thought he was doing well. I guess I thought wrong. How will Adella handle the news? How soon can I get to Azariah? Is this really my life?

We were less than a block away from my sister's house when I received a text from Adella that read: "Mom, is what Azariah is saying about dad true?"

At that very moment, a red garbage truck pulled out in front of us, completely blocking the road. Without even thinking, I kicked off my shoes, opened the door, and began sprinting down the street as Josh shouted, "Ashley, we're almost there."

I burst into my sister's house, raced up the stairs, and ran to Adella. She was in total disbelief and too shocked to cry. And suddenly, time seemed to stand still. I froze as if the world had stopped spinning. Grabbing Adella in a tight hug, I whispered, "I'm so, so sorry. I love you."

My sister rushed home from work to watch the kids. Later that day, Josh booked me a flight. The chaos of life ensued, but I knew I was made for this just like the waves are made to rise and fall. That is, after the initial shock wore off.

There was so much to sort out in the coming days and weeks, but first things first: I had to get to my son.

Josh booked flights for Azariah and me last minute, so they weren't ideal. The first—from Nashville to Chicago O'Hare, then to the U.S. Virgin Islands—felt like the longest I'd ever taken. As I traveled, I texted people to update them about Ryan and to ask for their prayers. During that journey, Ryan's other ex-wife, Evelina, and I exchanged texts about the situation. Since her first language was Spanish, and I spoke little to none, we stuck to texting. She explained that, based on the scene at the house, it appeared to be a drug-related death. Until the autopsy was completed, we would not know for sure. With Ryan's history of addiction, we couldn't help but assume.

I arrived several hours before our return flight was scheduled to take off. Evelina was going to bring Azariah to the airport for me. Thank God she lived near Ryan and Azariah. When crisis hits, you can always count on another mom to step up for your kids, no matter how many differences or how much personal disdain there might be. She had agreed to take Azariah overnight and bring him to the airport in the morning for our flight.

While I waited for them to arrive, I found a spot on the hard tile floor to sleep. I was exhausted from my red-eye flight, and we landed just before 5:00 a.m. According to my Oura ring, I had managed only fifty-six minutes of sleep. The airport floor was neither comfortable nor clean, but I didn't care—I took off my sweatshirt, laid it on the floor, and leaned against the wall in a desperate attempt to get whatever sleep might come my way before Azariah and Evelina arrived.

Eventually, Starbucks opened, so I abandoned the idea of sleep and opted for coffee instead. I was going to need a lot to get through the day. A few hours later, Evelina let me know they were pulling up and I should go outside to grab Azariah.

He got out of the car and sauntered over to the sidewalk. He looked tired. I embraced him in a long hug with a smile on my face and tears in my eyes. A mother's worst nightmare is being unable to help her son when he's thousands of miles away and in need. He seemed shaken, but okay. It was time to go home.

We went through security, boarded a plane, and headed home on an unnerving eighteen-hour three-leg trip: Miami, Chicago, and finally Nashville. We wanted to get home as soon as possible, and they were the only flights with two seats remaining.

God, is this nightmare over yet?

Several weeks later, Ryan's family set a date for the funeral. They asked me to help get the word out, so I took to social media to spread the news.

"Do you want me to go to your dad's funeral?" I cautiously asked Adella and Azariah, anxiously awaiting their response. "It's completely up to you. My feelings won't be hurt if you want me to stay home."

"What do you mean? Of course we want you to go," Adella replied, "You're our mom."

"Yes mom. We want you to go," Azariah confirmed.

That type of grief felt weird. It differed from grieving Case's death. You grieve, but society almost tells you that you're not allowed to or that you can only grieve behind closed doors. After all, you're the ex-wife. I remember attending a funeral of a friend's dad in high school. His ex-wife was at the front of the line during family visitation. Boy, oh boy did the community talk—myself included. But now I understand, although the marriage failed, it didn't mean death was the next best option. There is a term for it—disenfranchised grief.

My dad and mom accompanied me to Ryan's funeral. Thank goodness, I hadn't seen most of his family since our divorce ten years prior, and I was nervous. Knots in my stomach, hives on my chest, I walked into the church. At least my parents accompanying me would give me someone to sit with and talk to. Sitting at Ryan's funeral, I'd never felt so internally uncomfortable in my entire life.

Why do I feel this way about a man I couldn't stand half of the time? With so much animosity, why is there still so much sadness?

He was a human, Ashley. A human being. He deserved to live.

The kids wanted to sit with Ryan's family while I sat with my mom and dad. I sobbed uncontrollably during the funeral processional as Ryan's family walked to their seats in the front row of the church. I feared my public grief would cause more harm than good. When Ryan's dad saw me as he was walking down the aisle, he stopped to embrace me. I was sure everyone in the church could hear my snorting cry. Love, acceptance, forgiveness, sorrow, and maybe a little anger all wrapped up in a single hug. I knew it was important for me to be there for my kids, but I didn't know until I was there how important it was for me too.

After the service, Ryan's family welcomed me with open arms. Hug after hug, they thanked me for being there for the kids and asked how we were all doing. A piece of my heart, broken after the divorce, began to heal. I needed that healing.

Disenfranchised grief is so odd. It is impossible to put into words.

Ryan's death seemed to consume every conversation I had with Josh—hardly the topic a newly married couple envisions dominating their daily lives. Yet, that's what grief does. It consumes you. Our thirty-minute morning walks, which were once filled with light-hearted conversation and planning for the future, became weighed down by death. Insurance, retirement accounts, legal paperwork—the business of dying had taken over our lives. Underneath it all, there was the disbelief, the grief, the attempt to process something that still didn't feel real. For now, the logistics of death took precedence to coping with it.

I am sure it had to be weird for Josh, and I didn't know what to share and what not to share as I processed through my disenfranchised grief. Imagining him being in my shoes and me in his, I would share what felt appropriate from that vantage point. But sometimes I had to share, even if it hurt.

For me, talking was my way to cope, my way to feel seen and heard, my way to process the unbearable. But for Josh, talking about Ryan was confusing, even frustrating. In the wake of Ryan's death, he was suddenly hearing a completely unique version of the man he knew through my stories. Instead of the tumultuous, addiction-ridden Ryan—the man whose struggles had wreaked havoc on my life—he was now being introduced to the charismatic, fun-loving, larger-than-life version of Ryan, the guy who could charm anyone in the room and make people laugh until they cried.

It made little sense. How could those two versions of the same person exist?

But the truth was, they could. And they did. Both were real.

Six months after his passing, fentanyl intoxication was cited as Ryan's cause of death. I felt both a tremendous amount of guilt and an incredible amount of empathy in Ryan's passing, knowing what it's like living in the dark world of addiction, and feeling as though, in part, my marriage-ending affair caused his demise. Deep down, I knew I hadn't single handedly caused his death. I knew it was his addiction that ultimately took his life. But the reason behind it didn't matter. It was a tragic loss for loved ones and an incomprehensible loss for my kids.

There's a reason they say addiction is cunning, baffling, and powerful—because it is.[7] And in that, I felt a great sense of empathy for Ryan because I understood just how cunning, baffling, and powerful it could be. So cunning, it almost took me down. So baffling I couldn't comprehend how I'd gotten to the depths of despair I had. So powerful it almost ended my life, before it took his.

Several months after Ryan had passed away, while enjoying our morning walk, I asked Josh, "Is this what you thought you were getting into when I asked, 'Are you sure you're ready for this?'"

He immediately replied, "Absolutely not!"

I laughed—dark humor was my way of coping. Some things in life are simply beyond preparation, no matter how hard you try.

To help Azariah cope with the trauma of his experience, we enrolled him in a year-long counseling and school program for boys. Josh and I started couples counseling—after all, we had endured more in the first several months of our marriage than many marriages face in a lifetime. We spent more time and money on therapy than we'd like to admit—but every dollar was a dollar well spent.

Aside from death and counseling programs, blending our families came with its own set of challenges—navigating different parenting styles, schedules, and emotions—but it also brought unexpected joys as we began building new traditions together.

CHAPTER 26

THE SONG

Coordinating Christmas with five kids—who are loved by even more families—is anything but easy. Add in multiple dominant personalities, each convinced their festivities should take priority, and it becomes downright impossible. After struggling to find a date to celebrate Christmas in 2023, we knew, for the rest of our lives, we'd have to be okay celebrating on non-traditional days in non-traditional ways. That year, we settled on celebrating Christmas with all seven of us on December 14, 2024. Though unconventional, we decided that Christmas was what you made it. Blended family life *isn't* for the faint of heart.

The kids exchanged gifts. We had given them each $25 to carefully select a present for each of their siblings. We laughed as wrapping paper was tossed across the living room as the kids frantically opened their gifts. After gifts, we sat at our kitchen table, not quite big enough for seven people, and devoured steaming hot Papa Murphy's pizza. Then, we piled into the car for a surprise—an escape room. Josh may have let the cat out of the bag earlier that week, but half of the kids had never been to an escape room, so they didn't know what to expect. Some might call it crazy to voluntarily lock ourselves in a room for an hour with five kids, and crazy we were!

"I call DJ." Adella said, grabbing the middle seat before anyone could contest.

Josh, surprisingly, agreed. "Okay."

I raised an eyebrow. *Shocking. He never lets the kids be DJ.* I smiled to myself as we continued down the road. This was going to be a ton of fun or a total disaster, but more likely a slight mix of both.

The first song was definitely not kid-appropriate. Adella quickly skipped to the next.

Three-inch heels on our first date

Hugged me close against your chest

"Aww," I cooed, already lost in the slightly cheesy lyrics, thinking back to my first date with Josh, as I turned to ask the kids how quickly they thought we'd escape the room.

Back and forth to Mexico

Whales and dolphins too

On that sunset beach in Cabo

You said "yes" 'neath skies of blue

"Oh my goodness!" I shrieked a little too loudly for the acoustics of the car, smacking Josh's arm. "Did you have this song written for us?"

He glanced over, smiling, and reached for my hand, squeezing it.

From Tennessee to Horseshoe Bend

We brought everyone along

If what they say is true 'bout strength in numbers

Then honey, this family is strong[7]

At that moment, Josh spoke the language of my heart—music. My heart was filled with gratitude. Through all the craziness, the difficulties, the moments when life felt too busy to catch a breath, that moment was enough. The meticulous thought of every word. The country twang in the song. The lyrics that spoke to my heart. At that moment, our family listening to that song in the car was enough.

Pulling into the parking lot, the kids practically bounced out of their seats, buzzing with excitement.

"Alright, listen up," I said, attempting to calm the chaos. "If we don't work together, we don't escape."

"It's gonna be easy," Lucas, Josh's youngest son, said as he rolled his eyes.

"We'll see about that," Josh smiled as he leaned over and whispered, "This is going to be interesting. A battle of dominant personalities. We'll see who takes the lead."

I took it as a subtle hint to not take over.

Once inside, the escape master led us to the room we had reserved—Shanghai Spy. It was designed like an old hotel room. It was brightly lit, barely furnished, yet filled with hidden clues and codes. A large map covered the table, two chairs were pushed against it, and a telegraph sat on the windowsill. A rug partially covered the floor, and in the corner sat an old black suitcase with a lock on it. The room was emptier than I had anticipated.

We anxiously watched the introductory video while the younger kids scanned the room, already looking for clues.

"Pay close attention to dates, and don't pick the locks," the video wrapped-up.

The timer started counting down: 60:00.

Silence.

"What now?" I asked.

"Well, this is underwhelming," Azariah muttered, glancing around. "What are we trying to do here?"

"Start looking for clues," Josh said.

"What clues? I've never done this before." Azariah looked at me and shrugged.

"Let's split up," Adella suggested. "Check everything."

And just like that, it was mass chaos. No one knew what they were doing. No one had a plan, but we all set out to find the clues and hopefully our way out of the room.

Josh and Lucas sat at the table and hovered over the map. They traced their fingers over the streets and looked for patterns in the coordinates.

Waverly and Azariah were immediately intrigued by the telegraph. Waverly pressed the button again and again. It clicked and buzzed with every tap.

"Stop," said Azariah, nudging Waverly softly. "You're supposed to spell something, not just tap randomly. You're going to mess it up."

"But I think this thing actually works," Waverly whispered. Her eyes were wide with excitement even though she had no idea what was going on.

As they fiddled around with the telegraph, Braxton, Josh's oldest son, knelt beside the suitcase, messing with the lock. "I bet there's a clue in here," he whispered to himself.

Don't pick the locks. I resisted the urge to take over.

We went through item after item in the room. We uncovered hidden messages on the map, deciphered receipts stuffed inside the suitcase, and slowly pieced together the CIA-themed mystery designed for a minimum of six players.

The tension in the room grew as our time counted down. I still had no idea what was going on or what we were trying to do, but I took Josh's subtle hint and stayed away from leading the room. It's hard to lead when you don't know what you're doing.

I glanced at the clock—50:00 left.

Josh and Lucas eventually found a hidden code on the dates on the receipts tied to the map coordinates. This opened a door to a dimly lit second room. The space was small—barely large enough for three of us.

Azariah found two black light flashlights and handed one to Waverly.

"I feel like an actual spy," she giggled, shining the light in Azariah's eyes.

"Stop it," he said. "You're blinding me. And time is running out."

Adella and I tackled the map in the second room, scanning frantically for hidden words or patterns.

We were falling behind, so we decided to get a clue. Our clue was, "The word you're looking for is only four letters long."

"Try park," I yelled to Azariah, who was still at the telegraph.

He punched in the Morse code for the letters P-A-R-K.

A hidden door swung open.

"Yes!" We all cheered.

Inside was a long list of codes.

"But what does it mean?" Lucas asked, scanning the paper.

The timer now read 02:30.

Braxton was already one step ahead, recognizing a pattern between the codes and the colors he'd spotted on the map. Frantically, Josh entered one sequence after another as Braxton shouted codes. We knew we only had five attempts to get it right. The tension grew.

Five seconds left.

"0497! 0497! 0497!" Braxton shouted as Josh punched in the numbers.

CLICK. The lock popped open. We were one second late, but a wave of cheers erupted anyway. When the escape master entered the room, he gave us the win.

"We did it," Waverly said as a smile spread across her face.

"Barely." I laughed, still catching my breath from all the excitement.

The best part was that we escaped without any meltdowns or arguments.

Christmas 2024 was complete, and a new family tradition started.

CHAPTER 27

THE UNWRITTEN

On May 9, 2025, we hosted Adella's graduation party at a local golf country club. As I was checking out at the local drugstore, picking up a few remaining items, I glanced at the flower case in front of me. There was a light purple vase, filled with dark purple carnations, white daisies, yellow irises, and purple babies' breath. Purple was Ryan's favorite color. I knew I had to get the flowers.

"Are those reserved for someone?" I asked politely.

The woman glanced over at the case and shook her head. "No ma'am. They're yours if you want them."

Walking into the parking lot after purchasing the flowers, I burst into tears. Grief is like that. It hits you when you least expect it. I got into my car and tried pulling myself together on the short ride to the country club where the party was being held. It sucked that Ryan couldn't be there for our daughter's graduation. I couldn't imagine going through something like that as an eighteen-year-old.

When I arrived at the clubhouse, I found Adella's favorite picture of her and her dad. I took a black Sharpie and wrote,

"Sending love from heaven. - Dad." Her friends told me she was going to love it. I snapped a picture and texted it to her, giving her a heads up in case she felt strong emotions when she saw it. I didn't receive a response.

When she arrived at the clubhouse, she said, "Mom, why on earth would you send me that? I was at the middle school walk through, and I burst into tears in front of all of my friends." At least I knew she saw the meaning behind it.

The party was a tremendous success, and graduation was over before we knew it.

The flowers were a small wave of grace.

After two-plus years of married life, things are good, and sometimes things are messy. Josh and I argue; we are both bold, driven, and stubborn, always fighting for our way or opinion to rise above the rest. Just as Josh stepped into the role of bonus dad for my kids, I also had the privilege of becoming a part of his children's lives. It's been a learning experience for all of us, full of trial, error, and love. With five kids between us, our house is rarely quiet, and life is never boring.

Three are in taekwondo, one in competitive soccer, and one in competitive dance—our family calendar is fully booked! And then, there are the gut-wrenching moments: two of my kids grappling with the tremendous grief of losing their dad while also struggling to accept that he wasn't always the father they wanted, and trying to reconcile the presence of a stepdad who is there for them and wants to be seen as such.

It's hard. Busy. Agonizing. Fun. Joyful. Good.

Just the other day, one of my kids was suspended from school for three days for fighting—a reminder that healing isn't linear and life never stops being complicated.

Yet, amidst it all, there is tremendous joy. We don't get the good without the bad—every emotion holds an equally powerful counter emotion.

There are the small, everyday moments that make it all worthwhile—the ones where we collapse into laughter playing Cards Against Humanity until we're wiping away tears, or the endless rounds of Yahtzee and Exploding Kittens that turn into fierce competition. There's the pride that fills my heart when Adella, Azariah, or Braxton earn their next taekwondo belt, when Waverly beams from ear to ear on the dance floor, or when Lucas gets a hat trick in soccer. There's the joy of racing down water slides together on a weekend getaway as we turn every sporting event into a mini family adventure—savoring the moments we have together and doing our best to enjoy every wave that comes our way.

Waves have been a constant theme in my life—the relentless tides of grief, the turbulent storms of addiction, and, eventually, the quiet stillness that follows the storm. Sometimes the stillness is filled with joy. Sometimes it's filled with sorrow. Yet, no matter what, the same ocean that threatened to pull me under held the waves that eventually carried me forward.

The ocean's unpredictability, power, and capacity for destruction have *always* captivated me. It mirrors life in a way that nothing else does. The darkness beneath the surface encompasses a world of unknowns just like life, and the future holds a story that's yet untold. Just like the tides, life ebbs and flows. Sometimes, the waves crash down with such force that it seems nearly impossible to swim; other times, you grab a surfboard, catch a perfect wave, and ride it all the way in. Both experiences come from the same ocean—just as heartbreak and healing, grief and grace, and love and hate exist within the same story.

I carry this with me every day, etched permanently onto my arm. "He stilled the storm to a whisper. The waves of the sea were hushed." My life is a reminder that the waves will come and go—but I am never alone in the storm. Because for every tide of grief, there is always a wave of grace coming to carry me forward.

The rest, well—it's still unwritten.

"My grace is sufficient for you."

2 Corinthians 12:9

In memory of:

Cornelius John

February 28, 2008 – January 8, 2009

and

Ryan Antony

December 6, 1976 – June 5, 2023

Photo by Vanessa Bartels.

DEDICATIONS

TO MY READERS

Dear Readers,

My hope in writing these pages is that at least one person finds the strength and hope they need to carry on amid their own chaos—because if I can do it, so can you.

If that person is you, I am incredibly proud of you. Keep living, keep searching for those waves of grace, and when you see them, don't hesitate to ride. After all, what's the worst that can happen? You catch a wave, have a little fun, and maybe discover a new perspective on life.

I was recently talking with a friend as I prepared to finalize this book, and I told her how much I admire the bravery of people who share the darkest moments of their lives with complete strangers. She replied, "Some of their best moments too." And she was right—our worst moments can become our most cherished memories and sources of strength.

If nothing else, I hope you were at least entertained. Sharing my story brings purpose and meaning to my life, and I am so grateful that you're here, taking the time to read and walk this journey with me.

Thank you for laughing with me, for crying with me, and for sharing in the waves of grace that have carried me through. I am honored you took time to read my story. If you loved the story, please consider leaving an Amazon review. Your review will help the book reach more people in need.

Thank you,

Ashley Jo

TO CASE

Dear Case,

Writing this book brought tears to my eyes—especially the chapters about you. But as I wrote, and the tears fell to my keyboard, I thought about something that my Grandpa Gerry always used to say when we said goodbye to each other after a summer visit: "There wouldn't be so many tears if there wasn't so much love." And boy, oh boy, love is certainly something you've left etched on my heart.

Thank you for that love. I know today you're up in heaven, looking down on me, smiling, and I really hope you're proud. Sharing your story healed a piece of my heart that I didn't realize was broken.

Every year, when the anniversary of your passing arrives, I reflect on how your life and death have changed me. They both made me a better person. And even though it was some of the hardest shit I've ever been through, I am grateful for every single moment, every single breath, every doctor's appointment, and every tear.

It's hard to picture you as a seventeen-year-old because, in my heart, you will always be my baby boy with those beautiful brown eyes. Even though you were only here for ten months and ten days, I'll never forget your coo, your eyes, or your smile. I carry you with me every single day. You made me a better person.

Until we meet again, my sweet boy.

I'll see you in heaven.

Mom

TO ADELLA

Dear Adella,

Gosh, kiddo—where do I start? You are so incredibly strong, and I am beyond proud of the woman you've become. I'm so glad that my messy, chaotic life didn't ruin you completely. You turned out pretty damn good.

Above all, I am glad that we've been able to find our way through the crap that life brings, and through it all, that we've become friends. You are wise beyond your years—you're welcome. I feel like your life experience is the reason for your wisdom. I know you are going to do amazing things in life, no matter what you choose to do.

I'll never forget how fiercely you throw a punch—neither will my nose. Just make sure you only throw a punch when you really need to. And remember, when life knocks you down, because it will, I will be here.

Thanks for living through some of the hardest, yet most beautiful years of life with me. I love you more than words can say. And I am proud of you beyond belief. Keep doing great things.

Love always,

Mom

TO AZARIAH

Dear Azariah,

Last week you had your piano recital. As I sat and watched you play "Love Me, Love Me, Love Me," I was amazed at your dedication, your passion, and your talent. When you first set a goal to learn that song, I thought maybe you were setting the bar too high, but boy oh boy, you proved me wrong. When you put your mind to something, you accomplish it. Never forget that.

I'm glad that you love music too. We can always agree that music is the best, even when things get rough (and they have and will). Although you are young, you've experienced a lot of heartbreak, and I know I haven't always been the mom you've needed. I'm sorry. Thank you for showing me grace, even on the days I don't deserve it. I am so glad you got to spend a year with your dad and your brother in the U.S. Virgin Islands. Hold on to those memories for the rest of your life.

Whether you're skateboarding, snowboarding, meeting new friends, going for your personal best on the Rubik's cube, or playing the piano, whatever you do, keep smiling—your smile can light up the darkest room. Remember who you are, but more importantly, remember whose you are—a child of God.

As Psalm 93:4 (paraphrased) says, mightier than the waves of the sea is His love for you.

Never, ever forget that! I'm so glad God chose me to be your mom. And remember, whether you need advice, someone to vent to, or just to spend time together when life feels hard, I will always be here for you—no matter how old you are. It has been a wild and beautiful ride. I am proud of the young man you've become.

Love always,

Mom

TO WAVERLY

Dear Waverly,

I love you more than you know. Bringing you into this world reminded me of my resilience. Thank you. Now, every time I look at you, I see myself in you—your confidence, bold spirit, feisty personality, yet tender heart. Never stop being exactly who God made you to be.

Your dad and I hoped we could be a family one day, but life unfolded differently for us. Even though our story didn't end up the way we thought it would, that doesn't change how much we love you. It's a blessing for you to be loved, supported, and cared for by two incredible families. You have a mom, a dad, a bonus mom, and a bonus dad who would do anything for you. You have many siblings, and while they might annoy the heck out of you at times, they'll always support you and have your back.

When I watch you practice your dance and tumbling moves over and over again, I admire your determination. When I see you strike a pose on the dance floor, I admire your confidence. Never lose that spirit. The world will try to tell you to give up and that you are not enough, but don't let it. You are beautiful—inside and out. Shoot for the stars, and never stop being you. I know you are destined for great things.

I love you—so incredibly much.

Always,

Mom

TO JOSH

Dear Josh,

Even though I've shared every story in this book with you—from our third date onward (yes, maybe I'm an over-sharer)—I still can't imagine what it must be like to read these pages, written with all their raw passion and color. I've always been good at keeping you on your toes, and I'm sure this book did the same. Thank you for never asking me to filter my truth for your sake. If I had, we'd probably be missing all the juicy details that make this story entertaining.

Your ongoing, unwavering support allowed me to complete this book, and this book brought healing to my heart. Thank you for putting up with my stubbornness and uncanny attitude, even when it meant dragging you into therapy sessions to wade through the shit with me. You've been my friend, my partner in crime, and the person who presses me to reach new heights—literally since I'm deathly afraid of heights. I'm forever grateful that you love my kids as if they were your own and that you said "yes" when I asked if you were really ready for all of this. I also appreciate your willingness to compromise and use a curtain as a wall.

As one of our mentors said, "There's a reason Psalm 119:105 says, 'Your word is a lamp for my feet, a light on my path.' If we knew the entire journey, we wouldn't take the steps." Your faith in us, even when I was busy stumbling through life, has helped me find my way. Thank you for joining me on this wild ride—pushing me out of my comfort zone, challenging me, and most importantly (please sense my sarcasm), taking me to Cabo to see the whales.

I love you,

Ashley Jo

TO MY FAMILY

Dear Family,

Thank you for loving me and for being my eyes when I couldn't see. (Just kidding—I saw the moment and I took it!) But truly, thank you for always loving me, supporting me, and putting up with me.

When I kept some of you at arm's length at times, please know it was me, not you. No matter the distance, I know that if I ever called, you'd be there—like a lifeline, steady and strong. Thank you for being amazing.

Josh's family—you all are so much fun. Thank you for welcoming me into the family.

Mom and Dad, thank you for raising me in a family where God was at the center. When I was lost, that was the light that helped me find my way.

Kelsey, thank you for always being honest—even when it hurts.

Dani, thank you for loving me, even when I'm difficult.

Robyn, thank you for picking me up when I fell down the hardest.

Jory, you're welcome—my kid is the reason you're married.

Matt, thank you for giving me fun when I needed it most.

Kyle, just thanks. You rock.

I love you all,
Ashley Jo

TO RYAN

Dear Ryan,

Before writing this book, I had forgotten about the good in you. The pain, the grief, the hurt, and the heartbreak clouded my mind. This book reminded me of the fun, charismatic man I once knew and loved—the one who could make a room erupt in laughter and lead with a faith so bold it was impossible to deny.

I will always be grateful for your grace, compassion, and understanding during my battle with alcohol. During moments of withdrawal, when I truly thought I was dying, you reminded me again and again that I would survive. And you were right. You were the first person to teach me what recovery looked like—years before I needed it. You introduced me to the program that eventually saved my life. For that, I will always be grateful.

The first time you walked up to someone in the grocery store and asked if you could get your favorite apples at a lower price, I was appalled. But when I saw that it actually worked, I was amazed. Your courage and confidence taught me a lesson I still carry with me today—it never hurts to ask. If the answer is no, you're no worse off than when you started.

When you grew your beard, dressed like Jesus, and carried a life-sized cross down the streets of our city, I admired your faith and conviction. When reporters stopped to ask for your name, and you refused to share it because this wasn't about you, I knew your faith was real. You prayed with strangers, worshipped with your arms stretched wide, and invited the new person at church into our life group without hesitation. Your fearless spirit helped give me confidence.

Our kids are resilient, just like us. They love you with all their hearts. I tell them the age-appropriate truth—the stories in this book, the struggles you faced, and the good stories too. No matter what, they will always love you.

I'm sorry that life on this earth was hard for you. I'm sorry I had an affair. I'm sorry that you couldn't overcome addiction. I understand you now in ways I never could when we were together. And though our journey was filled with heartache, I am deeply grateful for the person I have become. After a lot of money on therapy and many hours at church, I have learned to forgive you. I hope, in the moments before you left this world, that you found it in your heart to forgive me too.

I believe in the faith you once held so dearly. Reading your pardon letters while writing this book reminded me just how real it was. And on the day you died, a part of me ached with jealousy that you got to see Case before I did. Please, hold him tight.

Your struggle does not define you. Those who knew you, knew you. They saw your battle, and they loved you anyway. Thank you, Ryan, for everything—the lessons, the pain, the laughter, and the love. I know we'll see each other again.

Ashley Jo

AFTERWORD

Joshua Tyler

R eading Ashley's book sparked feelings and emotions about
our journey that felt like tides and waves in itself. It brought
joy, anger, frustration, but most importantly, perspective. I see
the world differently and appreciate the deep conversations as
we navigate the chaos together.

I am proud of her for courageously sharing her story. If
we are being honest, few of us are brave enough to vulnerably
share ours. She unapologetically put herself out there and her
story has an immediate impact on anyone who hears it. For
those who have had the privilege to have Ashley in their life,
you know she is fiercely passionate about her kids, her family,
and the health and well-being of others. She is also stubborn as
hell, so be prepared if you ever decide to go toe to toe with her.
I will bring the popcorn.

There were many things about Ashley I fell in love with, but
the one that leaves me in awe is her unwavering faith in Jesus.
Psalms 107:29 is tattooed on her arm:

"He stilled the storm to a whisper; the waves of the sea
were hushed."

That is a calming reminder to stay grounded in our faith.
As I reflect on her story, and now our journey together, we are

at our best when faith is at the core of our life. I would like to think we have endured the worst of the storm, but that hasn't been our reality, and yet, I am at peace with whatever storm is thrown at us. I know we will figure it out and continue to raise our five kids the best we know how to.

Ashley, thank you for the impact you have had on my life, thank you for the passion you have for our family, and thank you for being the badass you are. I love you and am looking forward to this next voyage life has in store for us.

LOVE THE STORY? HEAR THE SOUNDTRACK.

My entire life, music has been my lifeline. The
songs shared throughout this story kept me
going during my most difficult storms.

Though I couldn't include every lyric, I created a
playlist to keep the spirit of the music alive.

You can revisit certain moments or simply sit and listen. The
Tides of Grief, Waves of Grace playlist is my gift to you.

thisisashleyjo.com/playlist

NOTES

1. U.S. National Library of Medicine, "DailyMed - Methadone Hydrochloride Tablet," last modified June 13, 2022, https://dailymed.nlm.nih.gov/dailymed/drugInfo.cfm?setid=aa8e14c1-fbfd-4e4d-b59e-2d4ae1ca815f.

2. Boston Children's Hospital, "Spinal Muscular Atrophy (SMA)," accessed July 31, 2025, https://www.childrenshospital.org/conditions/spinal-muscular-atrophy-sma.

3. Pierce Burr and Anil Kumar Reddy Reddivari, "Spinal Muscle Atrophy," StatPearls, NCBI Bookshelf, July 17, 2023, https://www.ncbi.nlm.nih.gov/books/NBK560687/.

4. Cleveland Clinic, "Spinal Muscular Atrophy (SMA)," last modified June 2, 2025, https://my.clevelandclinic.org/health/diseases/14505-spinal-muscular-atrophy-sma.

5. Lauren Dunn and Linda Carroll, "$2.1 Million Drug to Treat Rare Genetic Disease Approved by FDA," NBCNews.com, May 24, 2019, https://www.nbcnews.com/news/amp/ncna1009956.

6. Daniel J. Siegel, *The Developing Mind: How Relationships and the Brain Interact to Shape Who We Are*, 3rd ed. (New York: Guilford Press, 2020).

7. *Alcoholics Anonymous: The Story of How Many Thousands of Men and Women Have Recovered from Alcoholism*, 4th ed. (Alcoholics Anonymous World Services, 2001), 58.

8. Rob Lindquist, "All Part of the Plan," performed and produced by Rob Lindquist, SongFinch, 2024, Spotify, https://open.spotify.com/track/2CI0lhKGTqrwtxZ2YVVX8U?si=HfF8dtjJTh-qoUvx_3_4oQ.

ABOUT THE AUTHOR

ASHLEY JO is a sober mom, wife, and executive. With six kids and thirty employees, every day is a balancing act, one she navigates with fierce intentionality. What began as a way to process her son's illness through journaling quickly became a passion for writing and navigating life's twists and turns. By day, she leads a high-performing team. By night, she's home for dinner and "happy-crappy" with her family before the never-ending cycle of evening activities. She's proof that you can love Jesus, curse a little, and get back up every time life knocks you down.

thisisashleyjo.com

Instagram: @thisisashleyjo